SPICE
KITCHEN

SPICE KITCHEN

Ragini Dey

From the Ganges to Goa:
fresh Indian cuisine to make at home

hardie grant books
MELBOURNE · LONDON

CONTENTS

STORIES OF FLAVOUR & SPICE

Indian food is vibrant, colourful and richly flavoured; described by some as both God-like in its purity, yet devilishly sly as its spices lie in wait for unsuspecting palates. Its cuisine has diversified and strengthened throughout history by all those who have come into contact with it: The Ancient Greeks brought lamb and the art of cheese-making, the early Mughals came looking for land, victory, melons and grapes, yet introduced korma, biryani and the tandoor. Their descendants, with a penchant for lavish banquets, embraced India's spices, set up huge kitchen brigades, and helped develop the foundations of classical Indian cuisine. Under royal patronage, chefs experimented with different flavours and cooking styles, transforming ingredients to keep their masters' interest. With the coming of the Portuguese, Indian food gained complexity and heat – chillies, tomatoes and cashew nuts were all added to the Indian food repertoire. The arrival of the British Empire influenced Indian cuisine not with ingredients, but rather with new cooking techniques from English and French recipes.

Today, Indian food is truly global, influencing and being influenced by far-reaching corners of the world. Rustic meals, fine dining, street foods and regional specialties are all incorporated to make it one of the most exciting cuisines available.

My earliest food memories are of the family lunch table, specifically at my grandparents' home, where plates of kababs, curries, sweet seasonal vegetables, crunchy salads, crumbly breads, beautiful rice dishes, perky aachars (pickles) and chutneys, softened by velvety raitas were consumed, while mothers and fathers, aunts and uncles compared their favourite recipes and tips for making the best parathas. Everyone had their own little story to tell, while us kids just tried to sneak in one more gulab jamun, hoping no one was watching. These recipes were handed down through the years, forever adapting with each new generation.

I believe I am very fortunate to have been brought up in an environment that not only explored the regional tastes of my own neighbourhood, but those of the entire country. My immediate family loved to travel, and each holiday was spent in a different part of India where I was encouraged to sample unique foods and regional specialties. As a result, my cooking has always been influenced by multi-regional flavours, many of which I have fine-tuned in my restaurant, and the resulting recipes can be seen in this book. Over the last twenty years at the Spice Kitchen, many of the more traditional recipes have gained star status by combining flavours of the north, south, east and west to produce innovative, multi-layered dishes that complement each other. You too can make up your own menu by pairing recipes from the various chapters in this book. Do not be constrained by regions and tradition, but instead be guided by the flavours and variety of dishes available.

Is Indian food difficult to cook? Not at all – it is just a matter of learning the rules before breaking them! The recipes presented here are authentic and easy; some have an interesting twist, and all can be prepared with readily available ingredients.

To really enjoy your Indian meal, aim for a balance of meat and vegetable dishes, rich and simple, cooked and raw, hot and cold; accompanied by rice, bread, salad, chutneys and pickles. Alternatively, take advantage of the vast array of vegetarian dishes on offer – one of the most distinctive elements of Indian cuisine is the predominance and importance of vegetarian food.

An Indian kitchen is a fragrant kitchen. The aroma of spices permeates every part of the body and soul, nourishing and satisfying the palate. Spices and herbs are the foundation blocks of all Indian cuisine, and are certainly not restricted to traditional curries. In Indian hands, roasts are redolent of ginger, onion, bay leaf, cardamom, black peppercorns and mustard, while a simple fried fish might be marinated with fresh coriander, chilli, garlic, ajwaiin seeds and mace. As with all good recipes, balance is the key. Nothing illustrates the 'less is more' maxim better than the use of spices. Used individually, or in harmonious blends, spices bring perfection to any number of Indian dishes. On the other hand, there is nothing as terrible as a clumsily spiced dish with warring elements of sweet and bitter, or just muddied flavours. The careful blending of different spice quantities is always required to successfully achieve those few master dishes that use up to thirty-six spices.

Always start off with whole spices – seeds, fruit or bark. They have much more flavour than powdered varieties. Dry-roast or heat whole spices before grinding using a mortar and pestle or electric spice grinder to release their maximum flavour and taste. Stay away from mass-produced pre-mixed curry powders and pastes; apart from everything tasting the same, you will never be able to duplicate the freshness and intensity achieved with freshly blended spices where subtlety shines through alongside bolder, more vibrant tastes.

Don't be afraid to try unfamiliar spices to get to know their distinctive flavours. For vegetables or delicately flavoured ingredients, use only one or two spices to bring out the taste, such as onion seeds and chilli with cauliflower, or mustard seeds with fish. Experiment with different combinations – your imagination and taste buds will do the rest.

SPICES

Here is a guide to twenty of the most important spices used in Indian cooking.

Ajwaiin Seeds:

These tiny grey seeds come from the same family as cumin and parsley. In taste, they are similar to celery seeds with overtones of thyme. In Indian cooking, they are used to flavour deep-fried foods, fish and vegetables. Try ajwaiin seeds stir-fried with garlic, prawns (shrimp) tomatoes, coriander (cilantro) leaves and chilli.

Allspice:

This berry comes from the *Pimenta dioica*, a small tree native to the West Indies. The fruit is gathered when green and unripe and dried in the sun, where the berries turn black. Allspice has the flavour of cloves, cinnamon and nutmeg. It is also known as Jamaica pepper, and in India as *kababchini*.

Amchur:

Green mangoes are dried and ground to obtain this sour tangy spice, used to lift the taste of popular snacks such as samosas and pakoras. Amchur is especially useful if you want to achieve a sour taste like lemon or tamarind without the liquid content.

Asafoetida:

A very sharp-tasting spice derived from a resinous gum of the fennel family, asafoetida is used sparingly in vegetarian dishes and with lentils. North Indian recipes, especially from Kashmir, include asafoetida but always in very minute amounts. The gum is said to aid digestion and gives a unique taste, which you may either love or hate. Its aroma after cooking has been compared with that of truffles. For a simple recipe, add a tiny amount to hot ghee with julienned ginger and fresh green peas.

Cardamom:

Also known as the Queen of Spices, cardamom is the fruit of a reed-like plant from the mountains near the Malabar Coast in India. Two types are commonly used in Indian cooking: the small and more delicate green cardamom pods with thin black seeds inside, and the large brown cardamom pods, which are at least four times the size of the green. The pods release a beautiful fragrance when crushed and the seeds have a strong, sweetish flavour. Cardamom is an essential ingredient of garam masala (page 11), and is often used to flavour sweet dishes such as custards, ice creams and rice puddings.

Chillies:

In Indian cooking chillies are generally fresh green (unripe), dried red or ground as red chilli powder. The three cannot be interchanged in recipes as they all have different flavours. Fresh chillies also vary in pungency. A good guide is often the size: the smaller the chilli the hotter it is.

Cinnamon:

Cinnamon is the bark of an evergreen tree belonging to the laurel family, native to Sri Lanka, the Indian subcontinent, Malaysia and Indonesia. The outer bark is stripped away, and the inner bark is loosened and dried. Often confused with cassia bark, true cinnamon is softer and has a more subtle aroma. Cinnamon leaves are used to flavour curries, stocks and rice.

Cloves:

One of the oldest-known spices, cloves were regularly used by the Ancient Egyptians and the Romans. The clove (myrtle) tree can grow to heights of six metres and its unopened flower buds are carefully harvested. Known for its preservation qualities, cloves are used in both savoury and sweet Indian dishes.

Coriander:

The small round or oval brown seeds of the coriander plant are one of the most popularly used spices in Indian cooking. The seeds are usually roasted and ground before use. Fresh coriander (cilantro) leaves are used for flavouring curries, salads, chutneys and as a garnish.

Cumin:

Used either whole or as a powder, cumin is widely grown in Europe, India and Mexico. Cumin is said to stimulate the appetite and aid digestion. It is frequently used in curries, biscuits, couscous and fried rice. Fry whole cumin seeds in ghee and add to cooked vegetables, lentils and rice.

Fennel Seeds:

The dried fruit of a perennial herb of the parsley family, fennel is grown in Europe, India, the Middle East and Argentina. The seed resembles cumin in shape but is green and slightly fatter with a licorice-like flavour. Fennel is used whole and ground in breads, pickles, sauces, and in fish and South Indian meat curries. It is also an ingredient of the Indian five-spice mix, panch phoron (page 12). Cook rice with fennel seeds and whey for a really aromatic dish. Garnish with Indian panir cheese (page 13).

Fenugreek:

These squarish, yellowish-brown seeds have a slightly bitter flavour. They are used either whole or ground to flavour vegetables and curries. The leaves are used as a vegetable, and dried fenugreek is essential for certain recipes such as butter chicken. Add a few seeds to soup stocks or, with curry leaves, to vegetable soups for that special South Indian taste.

Mustard:

An ancient spice grown in most parts of the world, mustard seeds are used in both Western and Indian recipes. The pungency of the seeds is fully released when they are ground and mixed with water. In India, both the yellow and black seeds are used in cooking. Vindaloo is a popular example of a dish that uses mustard. Mustard oil, made from ground mustard seeds, is used widely in East and North India. Mustard seeds and mustard oil are used frequently when pickling fruits, and in vegetable and seafood dishes.

Nutmeg and Mace:

These two spices are from the same fruit grown in Malaysia, the Indian subcontinent, Indonesia and the West Indies. Nutmeg is the seed, protected by a thin shell. The shell has a coat of orange flesh which, when dried, becomes mace. Although the aroma of mace is similar to that of nutmeg, mace is sweeter. Nutmeg is used finely grated in sweets, curries and sauces, while mace is coarsely crushed and used

to flavour soups and stocks, as well as sweet dishes and rich Mughal curries and biryanis. When buying nutmeg choose seeds that are round, compact, have an oily appearance and feel heavy for their size.

Onion Seeds:

Sometimes known as black cumin, these tiny black seeds have a sweet flavour. An ingredient of the Indian five-spice mix, panch phoron (page 12), onion seeds are also used as a pickling spice and to flavour breads.

Pepper:

The seeds or berries of the plant *Piper nigrum*, native to the Malabar Coast of India, are dried to make both black pepper (the whole berry) and white pepper (husk removed). Pepper is used whole, crushed coarsely or finely ground, and is also an ingredient of garam masala (page 11).

Poppy Seeds:

In India, white poppy seeds are mainly used for their nutty flavour and thickening quality when added to rich curries such as kormas and vegetables dishes. They are usually soaked in hot water for at least two hours and then ground to a paste. Add to cooked potatoes for a delicious vegetable accompaniment.

Saffron:

The world's most expensive spice is made from the dried stamens of a type of crocus that grows in the Mediterranean, the Middle East and India. A quarter of a million plants are required to yield 450 g (1 lb) of saffron. Buy only from reliable sources as fake saffron is often sold as a cheaper substitute. Saffron has an ethereal fragrance with a pale yellow colour and should be infused in warm milk to obtain the best results. Use in stocks, soups, rice and desserts.

Turmeric:

A ginger-like rhizome grown in India and the West Indies. In India it is usually dried whole and ground to a powder. The hard resinous flesh of the dried root varies from a dark orange to a deep reddish-brown. In its powder form it is usually bright yellow. Turmeric is not only used for its colour and flavour but also as a preservative.

BASICS

Indian cooking involves some basic recipes and techniques that you'll use again and again. There are page references to these basic recipes and techniques throughout the book. You'll find them quite simple, and they are worth learning because they will make a difference to the taste and texture of the dishes you cook. With them, your food will have that magical authentic Indian flavour.

Roasting and Grinding Whole Spices

Some recipes call for spices that are already ground. These recipes tend to require a subtler mix of flavours. Some recipes call for whole spices that then have to be ground freshly – the result is a greater freshness and a greater intensity of flavour. Then there are recipes that require whole spices to be roasted and ground. This is the process of dry-roasting, or dry-toasting, whole spices before grinding them. This intensifies the colour, flavour and aroma of the spices, and brings a greater richness and depth to the taste of the finished dish. Using spices that are already ground will save a bit of time, but they will not give the same result.

To dry-roast whole spices, heat a small frying pan over a medium heat. Add all the whole spices that the recipe requires to the pan and heat them gently, stirring continuously, until they are warmed through and have started to release their aroma. This should take about 2–5 minutes, depending on the quantity and type of spices you are working with. Take care not to overheat the spices, as this will destroy their colour and flavour. If the spices are too hot to touch, they have been burnt.

Remove the spices from the heat and leave to cool, then grind in an electric grinder or use a mortar and pestle to get the desired coarseness or fineness.

The word masala is a generic term that refers to a combination, or mix, of spices. The following spice mixes are commonly used blends.

Garam Masala
Makes 3 tablespoons

Garam masala has a very delicate flavour, so it's best to make it fresh every time you need it. The word garam means 'warm' and refers to the heating properties of the spices used in this blend. According to Ayurvedic medicine – a Hindu system of traditional medicine that originated in India – all spices are considered to be either heating or cooling, and you maintain an equilibrium of heating and cooling elements in the body by watching what you eat.

Garam masala is sometimes sprinkled on meat, fish or vegetable dishes right at the end of cooking.

3 teaspoons cumin seeds
1 teaspoon green cardamom pods
1 teaspoon black peppercorns
5 cm (2 in) cinnamon stick
1 teaspoon cloves

Heat a small frying pan over a medium heat. Add the spices and heat them gently, stirring continuously, for about 2 minutes, until they release their aroma. Cool, then transfer to an electric grinder or use a mortar and pestle and process to a fine powder. Use as directed in the recipe. Alternatively, you can store in an airtight container in the cupboard for 2 days, or in the refrigerator or freezer for a week, although it will lose some of its subtle aroma.

Chaat Masala
Makes 6 tablespoons

This is a piquant, tangy, sweet–spicy blend that is sprinkled on salads, starters and sliced or diced fruit – fruit chaat is a popular snack bought from street vendors in India. This particular spice blend stores well, so it can be made in advance or in larger quantities.

1 tablespoon cumin seeds
1 tablespoon black peppercorns
½ teaspoon cloves
½ tablespoon dried mint leaves
¼ teaspoon ajwain seeds
¼ teaspoon asafoetida
1 tablespoon rock salt
1 teaspoon ground amchur
1 teaspoon ground ginger
1 teaspoon chilli powder

Heat a small frying pan over a medium heat. Add the cumin, peppercorns, cloves, dried mint, ajwain seeds and asafoetida and heat gently, stirring continuously, for about 1 minute, or until they release their aroma. Cool, then transfer to an electric grinder or a mortar and pestle. Add the salt, amchur, ginger and chilli and process to a fine powder. Use as directed in the recipe, or store in an airtight container in the cupboard for up to 3 months.

Balti Masala
Makes 5 tablespoons

This spice mix gets its name from the cast-iron bucket, known as a balti, that was originally used to cook balti-style dishes. The karahi (a small Indian wok) has now replaced the bucket! Add to meat, seafood or vegetable dishes while stir-frying over a high heat for the distinctive bold taste of balti cooking.

1 teaspoon chilli flakes
2 tablespoons coriander seeds
1 teaspoon black peppercorns
2.5 cm (1 in) cinnamon stick
½ teaspoon cloves
½ teaspoon green cardamom pods
1 teaspoon dried fenugreek leaves

Put all the spices in an electric grinder or use a mortar and pestle and process until coarsely crushed or ground. Use as directed in the recipe, or store in an airtight container in the cupboard for up to 1 month.

Panch Phoron
Makes 2 tablespoons

Here is a spice mix from Bengal that uses whole spices rather than spices that have been crushed or ground. It is added early in the cooking process to fish and vegetable dishes. The contrasting and complementary flavours of the spices – pungent, bitter, sweet, astringent – bounce off each other to provide a special taste.

1 teaspoon black mustard seeds
1 teaspoon yellow mustard seeds
1 teaspoon fenugreek seeds
1 teaspoon fennel seeds
1 teaspoon nigella (kalonji)

Toss the whole spices together in a small bowl. Use as directed in the recipe, or store in an airtight container in the cupboard for up to 1 year.

Ginger Paste
Makes 250 g (9 oz/1 cup)

Indian dishes are never thickened with wheat flour – a real boon for those who are gluten-intolerant. Instead, sauces are thickened with other ingredients, which also add flavour. One of these is ginger paste, which gives body and a different taste from that obtained with grated ginger. It is important to use the preparation method stipulated in the recipe, as different methods give different results. Also, it is always better to make your own paste, as store-bought pastes often contain preservatives and additives that distort the flavour.

100 g (3½ oz) fresh ginger

Peel and chop the ginger. Process in a food processor with 125 ml (4 fl oz/½ cup) water to form a smooth paste. Use as directed in the recipe, or store in an airtight container in the refrigerator for up to 2 weeks.

Garlic Paste
Makes 250 g (9 oz/1 cup)

Along with ginger paste, garlic paste is commonly used to thicken sauces. It results in a smoother texture and subtler flavour than chopped or crushed garlic, which gives a different, fresher taste and more coarsely textured sauce.

100 g (3½ oz) garlic cloves

Peel and chop the garlic. Process in a food processor with 125 ml (4 fl oz/½ cup) water to form a smooth paste. Use as directed in the recipe, or store in an airtight container in the refrigerator for up to 2 weeks.

Saffron Infusion
Makes 2 tablespoons

Using an infusion of saffron threads in milk distributes the saffron flavour more evenly and strongly during cooking than simply adding the saffron threads to the pan. The infusion must be made fresh, so reduce the amount you make if the recipe requires less.

3 saffron threads
2 tablespoons milk

Gently heat the saffron and milk in a small saucepan over a low heat for 2 minutes. Remove from the heat and leave to stand for 20 minutes to let the flavour develop and intensify. Use as directed in the recipe.

Ghee
Makes 500 g (1 lb 2 oz)

Ghee is clarified butter or cream. It is used extensively in Indian cooking for sautéing, frying, shallow-frying and even deep-frying. It is also added to dough or drizzled over a cooked dish or Indian bread just before serving to give a rich, nutty, buttery taste. Because it is clarified, it can be heated to higher temperatures than butter without burning.

You can buy ready-made ghee from Indian grocery stores. In some recipes you can use salted butter as a substitute for ghee, while in other recipes you can use vegetable or canola oil instead, but they will not bring the same rich flavour to the dish.

1 kg (2 lb 3 oz) unsalted butter or 1 litre (34 fl oz/4 cups) thick (double/heavy) cream

Heat the butter or cream in a large heavy-based saucepan over a low heat and simmer gently, uncovered and without stirring, for 1 hour. Remove from the heat and allow the residue to settle to the bottom, then decant the clear oil by pouring it very carefully into an airtight container. (The residue of crispy bits left in the bottom of the pan are considered a delicacy, and are delicious eaten with steamed rice.) The clear liquid will solidify when it is completely cool. Use as directed in the recipe, or store in an airtight container in the refrigerator for up to 6 months.

Panir Cheese
Makes 250 g (9 oz)

This fresh Indian cheese, known as chaana in Bengal, can be grilled, fried, braised or baked. It can be used in curries, stuffings, dips, snacks and desserts. Any kind of milk can be used to make panir, including goat's, sheep's and buffalo's milk as well as cow's. Different milks will give different textures. Full-cream milk, for example, will produce a softer and creamier panir. Different acid agents can be used to curdle, or separate, the milk and will also give a different texture. You could try lemon or lime juice, whey, yoghurt or buttermilk. The panir can be hung instead of pressed to give a different texture and consistency, suitable for desserts.

2 litres (68 fl oz/8 cups) milk
60 ml (2 fl oz/¼ cup) white vinegar

Line a large mesh strainer with a clean square of muslin (cheesecloth).

Put the milk in a large heavy-based saucepan over a medium heat and bring just to a boil. Remove from the heat and stir in the vinegar. Continue stirring just until the milk starts to separate, or curdle, and curds form. This should take about 1 minute.

Pour the liquid into the strainer lined with muslin, so that the whey drains away and the curds are caught in the muslin. Bring the corners of the muslin in to meet at the centre and tie in a knot. Transfer the bundle to a large bowl and sit a plate, that will fit inside the bowl, directly onto the bundle, weighted down with 2–3 cans. Leave for about 30 minutes, or until the panir is firm.

Remove the panir from the muslin and immerse it in a large bowl of cold water. Use as directed in the recipe. Alternatively, store it, covered in water, in an airtight container in the refrigerator for 5–7 days.

Tamarind Pulp
Makes 250 ml (8½ fl oz/1 cup)

Tamarind is a popular souring agent used in Indian cooking. In North India it is usually combined with something sweet, such as jaggery (dark brown unrefined sugar), molasses or sugar, to provide a sweet and sour flavour in dishes. In the west and south it is normally used in fish and vegetable preparations to add an intensely sour flavour. Tamarind is available in dried seedless form, as a concentrate or already pulped in refrigerated tubs. I prefer the dried tamarind that can be reconstituted into a pulp (as described here) when required, rather than the concentrate, which has an overly strong colour and flavour, or the ready-made pulp, which is perishable.

100 g (3½ oz) dried tamarind

Heat the dried tamarind and 250 ml (8½ fl oz/1 cup) water in a small saucepan over a medium heat, stirring occasionally, for about 3–5 minutes, or until the tamarind is softened and disintegrating. Strain through a mesh strainer into a bowl to obtain a smooth pulp. It will keep in an airtight container in the refrigerator for up to 2 weeks.

Fresh Coconut Milk
Makes 250 ml (8½ fl oz/1 cup)

Fresh coconut milk has a sweet flavour all its own. It also tends not to be oily. Although not as convenient as opening a can of coconut milk or cream, the recipes in this book will be vastly improved with fresh coconut. Freshly grated coconut is available from Asian grocery stores. Make sure it is not frozen as this tends to lessen the flavour. If it is not available and you need to grate your own, cut the white coconut flesh into large pieces and then grate with a grater. Alternatively, put in a food processor and use the grater attachment to process, or simply process with the blade attachment to chop finely.

100 g (3½ oz/2 cups) freshly grated coconut

Put the grated coconut in a large bowl, pour in 375 ml (12½ fl oz/1½ cups) hot water and steep for about 30 minutes. Line a mesh strainer with a clean square of muslin (cheesecloth) and strain the liquid through the muslin into a bowl underneath. Press down firmly on the grated coconut in the muslin-lined strainer to extract all the thick rich liquid from it. Use the coconut milk as directed, or store in an airtight container in the refrigerator for up to 3 days.

Note: Do not discard the grated coconut. Instead, use it to thicken curries, although be aware that it will not have a strong taste. Or you can use it to repeat the process of making fresh coconut milk up to three times. You will obtain first-, second- and third-strength coconut milk that can be added to recipes for strong or light flavour and richness.

Steamed or Boiled Rice
Serves 4

Steamed rice, especially steamed basmati rice, is the best complement for most curries. It is the everyday rice eaten in most Indian homes. North Indians prefer bread or biryanis and fried rice preparations. But while steamed rice is popular throughout India, it is deemed an insult to offer it to guests or serve it on festive occasions – it shows that the host did not take the trouble to serve something more elaborate.

200 g (7 oz/1 cup) basmati rice or other long-grain rice, washed and drained

To steam the rice, put it in a shallow heavy-based saucepan. Pour in 375 ml (12½ fl oz/1½ cups) water, stir and bring to a boil over a medium heat. Reduce the heat to low, cover and cook for about 20 minutes. Do not uncover or stir during the cooking time; this ensures that the rice cooks evenly and does not break up. Remove from the heat and, still covered, leave to rest for 10 minutes before serving. (This allows the rice grains to plump up to their maximum length.)

The rice can also be cooked by the boiling method. Put the rice and 1 litre (34 fl oz/4 cups) water in a large saucepan. Bring to a boil over a high heat, then reduce the heat to medium and cook uncovered for about 20 minutes, or until the rice is soft. Drain in a sieve but do not rinse in cold water.

The best steamed or boiled rice should be firm to the touch and al dente, not mushy.

Deep-frying

In India a karahi (Indian wok) is used for deep-frying, but a Chinese wok is a good alternative. The wok shape means that less oil is needed, compared with a saucepan. However, the rounded bottom of these woks is only safe to use on a gas stovetop. Special woks are available to use on induction stovetops and are very efficient. If you don't have a suitable wok you can use an electric deep-fryer.

Use any oil without a pronounced flavour, but that has a high smoke point, so that the oil can be heated to high temperatures without burning, spitting or giving off noxious fumes, and the food won't take on the particular flavour of the oil.

Different foods are deep-fried at different temperatures – the temperature of the oil can range from 160°C (320°F) to 210°C (410°F), depending on the item being cooked. For example, a samosa is deep-fried in oil heated to a medium heat (180°C/350°F) so the pastry cooks while the filling inside is only heated through. On the other hand, a crumbed vegetable patty needs the oil to be at a high heat (200°C/400°F) to cook all the way through. Breads such as pooris also need oil at a high heat (200–210°C/400–410°F) to make them puff out, and are fried for a very short time only – about 40–60 seconds. A thicker bread, such as a bhatura, needs slightly less heat (190–200°C/375–400°F) and is fried for longer – about 2 minutes – as it needs extra time to cook.

You can check that the oil has reached the correct temperature with a kitchen thermometer. Alternatively, drop 1 teaspoon of pastry, dough or batter in the oil. If it rises immediately to the surface, the oil is ready. If it settles at the bottom, the oil is not hot enough and the cooked food will be greasy. If the batter turns black, it is very hot and suitable for deep-frying breads but would burn very small items.

Avoid the temptation to fry too many items at once as this lowers the temperature of the oil and makes the food greasy. To avoid being splashed with hot oil, don't drop the items to be cooked in from a height. Instead, always put them on a slotted spoon or frying spoon, position the spoon as close as possible to the hot oil (being careful not to burn yourself) and let them slide in gently.

Pressure cooking

The modern pressure cooker is a boon to Indian cooking. While instructions for its use haven't been included in the recipe methods in this book, it can reduce the cooking time of certain dishes by about 75 per cent.

You can use a pressure cooker to make the cooking of lentils, dried beans and chickpeas a quick and easy task. After any necessary soaking and rinsing, put the lentils, beans or chickpeas in the pressure cooker with the specified amount of water and cook for one-quarter of the time specified in the recipe, or until they are the required softness.

Also consider using a pressure cooker for the lengthy tenderising part of cooking curries that use red meat on the bone, such as lamb shanks or beef or veal shanks (the cut of meat used for osso bucco); or secondary cuts of meat, such as lamb or goat forequarter or shoulder chops; or cheap stewing cuts of meat such as beef neck, chuck or brisket. Complete all the initial sautéing of onions, pastes and spices, browning of meat and stirring in of vegetables in a saucepan on the stovetop. Then transfer the mixture to the pressure cooker and simmer or cook gently for one-quarter of the time specified in the recipe, or until the meat is the required tenderness. If the curry needs to be finished with the addition of tempering, cream or any other ingredients, return the mixture to the saucepan, complete the final steps on the stovetop and serve. Otherwise, serve directly from the pressure cooker.

STARTERS &
SMALL BITES

In India, people love to snack throughout the day – morning tea, brunch, light lunch and afternoon tea, all provide an opportunity to bite into a samosa, break off a piece of bread and dip it into dal, salivate over a charcoal grilled kabab or enjoy the fresh crispness of a vegetable pakora – the list is endless. The recipes in this chapter come from all over India, and while the ingredients can change from region to region, the end result is the same – deliciously fresh and tasty dishes that satisfy the momentary appetite for something small.

Most Indian families do not eat a formal course-by-course meal, and many starters and small dishes are often incorporated into banquet-style meals. Perhaps start off with Masala Pappadums (page 22) and a couple of chutneys for dipping (see the Accompaniments chapter, pages 182–209), before moving on to traditional Pakoras (page 26) and Dahi Ke Kababs (page 37), served alongside larger fish and meat dishes. Recipes such as Vegetable Samosas (page 28) and Lentil and Prawn Wadas (page 44) work equally well served with pre-dinner drinks or as finger foods at a party, or even as a late-night snack after a night out.

Alternatively, try Swiss Brown Mushrooms with Akuri (page 38) for a breakfast with a twist, or indulge in the great combination of toasted buttery bread and vegetable dip – Pao Bhajee (page 32).

Many of the recipes in this chapter can be prepared ahead of time, which means you don't need to be in the kitchen when everyone else is enjoying them. So, sit back, relax and indulge in the tastiest small treats India has to offer.

Masala Pappadums

Serves 4 / Makes 8

This recipe takes the ubiquitous pappadum to the next level! The word pappadum comes from the Sanskrit 'parpata', meaning a kind of thin, crisp cake baked or fried in oil. Pappadums can be served with drinks or as an appetiser. In South India they are normally served with the main meal, crumbled and mixed with rice and curries to provide an exciting crunch. They can be made of lentils, sago, rice or potato. They are usually fried, although some brands can be cooked on a hotplate or under the grill (broiler).

250 ml (8½ fl oz/1 cup) vegetable or canola oil for shallow-frying

8 plain pappadums

2 tablespoons chopped coriander (cilantro) leaves

pinch of chilli powder

2 tablespoons chaat masala (page 11)

2 tablespoons desiccated (grated dried) coconut

Heat the oil in a wok or frying pan over a high heat until it is smoking. Cook 1 pappadum at a time for about 2–3 seconds, or until crisp. Remove from the frying pan immediately and place on a large tray. Repeat the process for the remaining pappadums.

Sprinkle the pappadums with the coriander, chilli powder, chaat masala and coconut. Serve immediately.

Note: You can also deep-fry the pappadums if you prefer. Heat 500 ml (17 fl oz/2 cups) oil in a wok or deep-fryer to 200°C (400°F) (see page 15), then continue as for the method above.

Prawn Curry Puffs

Serves 4 / Makes 12

My earliest memories of picnics in Kolkata (Calcutta), in the beautiful botanic gardens, or at the foot of a dam wall with water thundering nearby, cannot be separated from the never-forgotten taste of biting into a curry puff overflowing with fresh prawns (shrimp). This dish is an Anglo–Indian specialty. You can replace the prawns with minced (ground) meat or vegetables, if desired.

2 sheets ready-made shortcrust (pie) pastry

vegetable or canola oil for deep-frying

Filling

2 tablespoons vegetable or canola oil

1 tablespoon chopped onion

1 teaspoon garlic paste (page 12)

1 teaspoon ginger paste (page 12)

250 g (9 oz) raw prawns (shrimp), shelled and deveined, chopped

1 spring onion (scallion), chopped

1 tablespoon chopped green chilli

small handful coriander (cilantro) leaves, chopped

small handful mint leaves, chopped

½ teaspoon garam masala (page 11)

½–1 teaspoon salt, or to taste

To make the filling, heat the oil in a medium saucepan over a medium heat. Sauté the onion, stirring occasionally, for about 5 minutes, or until light brown. Stir in the ginger and garlic pastes and cook for 1 minute, then add the prawns and cook, stirring, for a further 2 minutes.

Add the spring onion, chilli, coriander, mint, garam masala and salt. Stir to mix through, then remove from the heat and allow to cool. If you are not using the mixture immediately, put it in the refrigerator.

Cut the sheets of pastry into twelve 5 cm (2 in) circles. Place a tablespoon of filling on one side of each pastry circle. Draw the other half of the pastry over the filling and seal firmly.

Heat the oil in a wok or deep-fryer to 180°C (350°F) (see page 15). Fry the curry puffs a few at a time for 6–8 minutes, or until golden brown.

Alternatively, you can bake the curry puffs. Preheat the oven to 200°C (400°F). Place the curry puffs on a greased, non-stick baking tray and cook in the oven for 15 minutes. Serve immediately.

Mushroom and Coconut Shorba

Serves 4

Soups were not traditionally served in India as a first course until the arrival of the British. However, soup-like drinks, both hot and cold, were sometimes served in tumblers throughout the meal. In South India pepper water and rasam (a spicy and acidic soup with tamarind juice as its base, said to be good for digestion) was popular, while in Rajasthan, yoghurt soups were traditionally served. North Indian soups are sometimes called shorba, which can also be another name for a thick sauce or gravy. This shorba – a combination of sweet and hot spices, mushrooms and coconut – is a really nourishing soup. Serve it hot with fresh crusty bread.

30 g (1 oz) salted butter

2 onions, sliced

360 g (12½ oz) button or cap mushrooms, cleaned and sliced

pinch of white pepper

½ teaspoon fennel seeds, ground

1 cm (½ in) cinnamon stick, ground

½ teaspoon cumin seeds, ground

2 green cardamom pods

½ teaspoon coriander seeds

250 ml (8½ fl oz/1 cup) fresh coconut milk (page 14) or canned coconut milk

1 teaspoon ginger paste (page 12)

125 ml (4 fl oz/½ cup) thick (double/heavy) cream

4 makrut (kaffir lime) leaves

½–1 teaspoon salt, or to taste

Heat the butter in a large saucepan over a medium heat. Sauté the onion for about 7 minutes, or until translucent. Add the mushrooms, white pepper, fennel, cinnamon, cumin, cardamom pods, coriander and 125 ml (4 fl oz/½ cup) of the coconut milk. Cook for 10 minutes over a low heat. Remove from the heat and allow to cool a little.

Purée the mixture in a food processor or with a hand-held blender. Return the purée to the saucepan, and stir through the remaining coconut milk, the ginger paste, cream and makrut leaves. Cook over a medium heat for about 6 minutes, or until the soup is heated through. Add the salt and serve hot.

Pakoras

Serves 4 / Makes 12–16

Quick to make and quick to eat, these crispy fried fritters are a popular finger food in India. This recipe is for the traditional pakora – the tempura-style individual piece of vegetable fried in batter. There are many types of pakoras, including prawn (shrimp), chicken, fish, bread and even hard-boiled egg! They are a really versatile snack to make when friends drop in unannounced, as you are sure to have at least one or two vegetables that you can use to dip in the batter. Pakoras are delicious served with Tamarind and Ginger Chutney (page 186) or Green Chutney (page 188).

250 g (9 oz) prepared mixed vegetables, choosing from the following:

200 g (7 oz) English spinach, stems discarded, individual leaves separated

1 small eggplant (aubergine), sliced into 2.5 cm (1 in) thick batons

1 large onion, sliced into thick rings

1 large potato, peeled and sliced into 5 mm (¼ in) rounds

4 cauliflower florets, broken into small florets about 2.5 cm (1 in) across

vegetable or canola oil for deep-frying

Batter

110 g (4 oz/1 cup) besan (chickpea flour)

1 teaspoon ajwaiin seeds

1 teaspoon chilli powder

2 teaspoons white vinegar

½–1 teaspoon salt, or to taste

To make the batter, mix together the besan, ajwaiin seeds, chilli powder, vinegar and salt in a medium bowl, then make a well in the centre. Gradually pour in 275 ml (9½ fl oz) water while whisking together the ingredients to form a batter that has a coating consistency – it should coat the back of the spoon and gently drip down. Stir in a little more water, if necessary, to achieve the right consistency.

Heat the oil in a wok or deep-fryer to 180°C (350°F) (see page 15). Dip the individual pieces of vegetable in the batter and deep-fry a few at a time until golden brown and cooked through – about 2–3 minutes for the spinach leaves, 4 minutes for the eggplant batons and onion rings, and 5 minutes for the potato rounds and cauliflower florets. Remove from the oil and drain on kitchen towels. Serve hot.

Vegetable Samosas

Serves 4

You can buy ready-made samosas – fried cone-shaped pastries usually filled with vegetables – at every corner shop in India. But the homemade version is much nicer and can be made in a range of sizes, depending on whether you want to serve them as cocktail nibbles or as a starter or lunch snack. Samosas can be filled with vegetables, meat, seafood or even chocolate! Serve these savoury vegetable versions with Green Chutney (page 188).

2 sheets ready-made shortcrust (pie) pastry

vegetable or canola oil for deep-frying

Filling

150 g (5½ oz/1 cup) diced mixed vegetables, choosing 4 of the following:

  1 small potato, peeled

  1 small carrot, peeled

  50 g (1¾ oz/¼ cup) corn kernels cut from the cob

  ½ small sweet potato, peeled

  6 green beans, trimmed

  40 g (1½ oz/¼ cup) shelled fresh or frozen peas

  2 cauliflower florets

1 tablespoon vegetable or canola oil

2 teaspoons ground cumin

2 teaspoons ground coriander

½ teaspoon chilli powder

½ teaspoon turmeric

½–1 teaspoon salt, or to taste

To make the filling, cook the vegetables of your choice in a medium saucepan of boiling salted water over a medium heat until they are just tender. As a guide, cook the potato for 4 minutes; add the carrot, corn and sweet potato and cook for a further 2 minutes; then add the beans, peas and cauliflower and cook for a final 2 minutes. Drain.

Heat the oil in a large frying pan over a medium heat. Add the cumin, coriander, chilli powder, turmeric, salt and cooked vegetables, mix together well and cook for about 1 minute. Remove from the heat and allow to cool.

Cut the sheets of pastry into ovals: make ovals 7.5 cm (3 in) in length for small samosas and ovals 15 cm (6 in) in length for large samosas. Now cut each oval in half across the width of the oval – you now have narrow hemisphere shapes of pastry. Fold the corners on the straight side of each hemisphere inwards. Lightly moisten the edges of each hemisphere with water, then bring the two edges to meet, pinch them together and shape the pastry into a cone. Place a little of the filling in each cone, then fold over the top of the pastry to cover the filling and seal the samosa.

Heat the oil in a wok or deep-fryer to 180°C (350°F) (see page 15). Fry a few samosas at a time until light brown and the pastry is cooked – about 5 minutes for small samosas and 7 minutes for large samosas. Drain on kitchen towels and serve hot.

Halim Lamb and cracked Wheat with Toast

Serves 4

Hyderabad, the capital of the state Andhra Pradesh in South India, has a fantastic food culture. Its kababs, biryanis and curries are world-renowned. I first tasted this famous Hyderabadi recipe at the exclusive Hyderabad Club. It shows off the versatility of Indian cooking and the influence of the Mughals. This is a special dish served during the Muslim month of Ramadan, the time of fasting. Lamb is the sacrificial meat traditionally used. It may be an ancient recipe, but halim lamb works really well as a contemporary dish, served as a warm dip with slices of toasted crusty bread.

100 g (3½ oz) minced (ground) lamb, preferably from the leg

100 g (3½ oz) cracked wheat

1½ tablespoons vegetable or canola oil

1 onion, sliced

2 green chillies

1 teaspoon ginger paste (page 12)

1 teaspoon garlic paste (page 12)

1 tablespoon chopped coriander (cilantro) leaves

1 tablespoon chopped mint leaves

1 teaspoon garam masala (page 11)

juice of 1 lemon

½–1 teaspoon salt, or to taste

8 slices sourdough or other crusty bread, toasted, to serve

Put the lamb, cracked wheat and 1 litre (34 fl oz/4 cups) water in a large saucepan. Cover with a lid and cook over a low heat for 2 hours, stirring regularly, until the meat is cooked through and the mixture looks like a thick sauce. Remove from the heat and set aside.

Heat the oil in a frying pan over a medium heat. Sauté the onion, stirring occasionally, for about 5 minutes, or until golden brown. Add the chillies, ginger and garlic pastes, coriander, mint and garam masala and cook for 2 minutes. Stir in the meat mixture and cook for a further 10 minutes.

Remove from the heat and blend with a hand-held blender until the mixture has a porridge-like consistency. Stir through the lemon juice and salt, and serve hot with the toasted bread.

Mulligatawny Soup

Serves 4

A really retro recipe, this dish is one of colonial India's favourite soups and it is still served in stuffy clubs and dingy hill station hotels. Full of lovely aromatic flavours, this British-influenced 'pepper water' is fabulously fragrant and will warm up the coldest evening. A true jewel in the Raj culinary crown!

250 g (9 oz) beef neck, chuck or brisket, diced

1 small onion, sliced

1 teaspoon ginger paste (page 12)

1 teaspoon garlic paste (page 12)

60 g (2 oz/¼ cup) split red lentils (masoor dal) or split yellow peas

1 carrot or turnip, peeled and diced

2½–5 cm (1–2 in) cinnamon stick

12 curry leaves

1 teaspoon turmeric

250 ml (8½ fl oz/1 cup) fresh coconut milk (page 14) or canned coconut milk

4 ripe tomatoes, chopped, or 400 g (14 oz) can diced tomatoes, drained

2 teaspoons each cumin and coriander seeds, roasted and ground (page 10)

¼ teaspoon fenugreek seeds, roasted and ground (page 10)

salt and freshly ground black pepper to taste

2 tablespoons lime juice

cooked rice (see page 14) (optional) to garnish

Fried Onions (page 209) to garnish

lemon or lime wedges to garnish

In a large saucepan or stockpot, combine the beef, onion, ginger and garlic pastes, lentils or peas, carrot or turnip, cinnamon, curry leaves and turmeric with 800 ml (27 fl oz) water. Bring to a boil over a medium heat, then lower the heat and simmer for 1 hour.

When the lentils are soft, stir in the coconut milk, tomato, cumin, coriander, fenugreek, and salt and pepper to taste, and cook for 15 minutes. Stir in the lime juice and cook for a further 5 minutes.

Serve hot, garnished with a little cooked rice if you have it available, fried onions and lemon or lime wedges.

Pao Bhajee

Serves 4

The Bollywood crowd queue up at Mumbai's specialist cafés and street carts for this favourite snack – a silky vegetable dip served with buttered toasted rolls. The Portuguese introduced yeast-type breads to western India in the sixteenth century. 'Pao' refers to small loaves of bread, and 'bhajee' is a selection of vegetables cooked on a hotplate with tomatoes and butter.

150 g (5½ oz) salted butter

2 tablespoons ginger paste
(page 12)

6 ripe tomatoes, chopped, or
1.5 x 400 g (14 oz) cans diced
tomatoes, drained

2 tablespoons garlic paste
(page 12)

4 large potatoes, peeled, boiled
and roughly mashed

2 teaspoons chilli powder

½–1 teaspoon salt, or to taste

small handful coriander
(cilantro) leaves, chopped,
plus extra to serve

1 teaspoon garam masala
(page 11)

8 small bread rolls, sliced in
half crosswise

lemon wedges to serve

Heat a heavy-based frying pan or a barbecue hotplate to a medium heat. Melt 75 g (2¾ oz) of the butter, then add the ginger paste and cook, stirring, for 5–10 seconds. Stir in the tomato and garlic paste and cook for about 8–10 minutes, or until the tomato has softened. Add the potato, chilli powder and salt and cook over a medium heat, stirring continuously, for about 10 minutes. Add the coriander and finally the garam masala and stir to mix through. Transfer the bhajee to a heatproof bowl.

Melt the remaining butter in the pan or on the hotplate. Add the bread rolls, cut side down, and cook over a medium heat for about 4–6 minutes, until they are brown and have soaked up the melted butter.

Serve the bread rolls topped with the bhajee and extra chopped coriander, plus the lemon wedges on the side. Alternatively, serve the bhajee in a bowl with the rolls on a serving platter, for scooping up the vegetable dip.

Onion Uthappams

Serves 4

Walk into a South Indian canteen or café during the early part of the day and you will be greeted by the sight of large hotplates with many variations of the uthappam being cooked to order. Uthappams – the word is derived from appam, which is a rice pancake – are South India's fantastic breakfast and brunch dish. These fermented rice and lentil pancakes are usually vegetarian, but at the Spice Kitchen we have added toppings such as eggs, prawns (shrimp), crab meat and roast duck for a special touch. Don't be put off by the time it takes to make the batter – once made, it can be left in the refrigerator for a week.

30 g (1 oz) ghee or salted butter or 2 tablespoons vegetable or canola oil

Coconut Chutney (page 188) to serve

Batter

225 g (8 oz/1 cup) parboiled (converted) rice or other short-grain rice

75 g (2½ oz) basmati rice or other long-grain rice

150 g (5½ oz/¾ cup) split white lentils (white urad dal)

½ teaspoon fenugreek seeds

1 red (Spanish) onion, chopped

2 green chillies, chopped

large handful coriander (cilantro) leaves, chopped

½–1 teaspoon salt, or to taste

To make the batter, rinse the parboiled and basmati rice and the lentils in cold water, then drain. Put in a large bowl with the fenugreek seeds and 2 litres (68 fl oz/8 cups) water, cover and soak overnight.

Drain the rice, lentils and fenugreek seeds, then process in a food processor to form a smooth batter that has the consistency of a thick soup. Pour into a clean large bowl, cover and keep in a warm place for 8–12 hours to allow the batter to ferment. When it is ready, it will have little bubbles on the surface and a slightly sour smell.

Add the onion, chilli, coriander and salt to the batter and mix together thoroughly.

Heat a heavy-based non-stick frying pan over a medium heat for about 2 minutes. Pour a small ladleful of batter into the pan and swirl it around to cover the base of the pan and form a thin pancake. Cook for about 4 minutes, or until bubbles appear on the surface. Add a little ghee, butter or oil around the edges of the pancake, then turn and cook the other side for a further 3 minutes, until golden brown and crunchy on the outside. Remove from the pan and serve with the coconut chutney.

Cabbage Bondas

Serves 4 / Makes 8–10

A very popular snack in Mumbai and its surrounding regions, bondas are round fritters made with besan (chickpea flour) and filled with potatoes. Sold from street carts or udipi cafés (vegetarian working-mens' canteens known for great-value, basic food), bondas are easily made at home. This version is not so well known but is delicious with the added crunch of cabbage.

75 g (2¾ oz) finely shredded white or red cabbage

1 tablespoon finely chopped onion

2 tablespoons finely chopped coriander (cilantro) leaves

1 teaspoon finely chopped green chilli

½ teaspoon turmeric

110 g (4 oz/1 cup) besan (chickpea flour)

½–1 teaspoon salt, or to taste

vegetable or canola oil for deep-frying

Coconut Chutney (page 188) to serve

Mix together the cabbage, onion, coriander, chilli, turmeric, besan and salt in a large bowl.

Add 60 ml (2 fl oz/¼ cup) water, 1 tablespoon at a time, and stir to combine until the mixture holds together firmly. (The amount of water required will depend on the type of besan you use, as some besans retain more liquid than others.) With wet hands, shape the mixture into flattened patties, about 1 cm (½ in) thick and 3 cm (1¼ in) in diameter.

Heat the oil in a wok or deep-fryer to 180°C (350°F) (see page 15). Deep-fry the patties, a few at a time, for about 4 minutes, or until crisp and golden brown. Drain on kitchen towels, and serve with the coconut chutney.

Note: The mixture can be stored in the refrigerator for up to 12 hours. During this time, water will seep out of the salted cabbage and make the mixture runny, so you may find that you do not need to add extra water before forming the mixture into patties.

Dahi ke kababs

Serves 3–4 / Makes 6–8

There is a huge repertoire of Indian kabab recipes, from meat patties and meat on the bone, to recipes that include vegetables and lentils. However, this unique, melt-in-the-mouth North Indian recipe, made from drained plain yoghurt, is outstanding. Yoghurt is a very popular ingredient throughout India and can take a starring role, as this recipe demonstrates. Serve the patties with a green salad and Tomato Chutney (page 194). They are also good as a starter or as part of an Indian banquet.

1 kg (2 lb 3 oz/4 cups) plain or thick Greek-style yoghurt

1 teaspoon finely chopped green chilli

1 tablespoon finely chopped coriander (cilantro) leaves

55 g (2 oz/½ cup) besan (chickpea flour)

½–1 teaspoon salt, or to taste

60 ml (2 fl oz/¼ cup) vegetable or canola oil

Put the yoghurt in the middle of a clean square of muslin (cheesecloth) resting in a bowl or container. Bring the corners in to meet at the centre and tie in a knot. Hang the bundle containing the yoghurt from a hook, put a container underneath to catch the draining whey, and leave to drain for 6–8 hours. In warmer weather, hang the bundle in the refrigerator.

Tip the drained yoghurt into a large bowl. Add the chilli, coriander, besan and salt and mix together well. With wet hands, shape the mixture into small patties about 2.5 cm (1 in) in diameter. (You should make 6–8 patties from this amount of mixture.)

Heat the oil in a heavy-based frying pan over a medium heat. Cook the patties, a few at a time, for about 2 minutes on each side, or until golden brown and crusty on the outside. Drain on kitchen towels and serve hot.

Swiss Brown Mushrooms with Akuri

Serves 4

Breakfast in India is never boring! Akuri is the Parsee version of scrambled eggs, eaten in western Indian cuisine. This recipe is a combination of spicy scrambled eggs and mushrooms. It can be combined with green peas or thinly sliced fried okra, or it is delicious on a bed of crisp-fried Straw Potatoes (page 209). Serve with good-quality bread, such as sourdough, Turkish flat bread or a baguette, or with Pooris (page 204) for a proper Indian breakfast.

8 large Swiss brown mushrooms or other flat mushrooms, such as field mushrooms, cleaned and stalks removed

1 tablespoon crushed black peppercorns

2 tablespoons sesame oil

6 large eggs

50 g (1¾ oz/⅓ cup) fresh or frozen peas

1 tablespoon chopped coriander (cilantro) leaves

1 teaspoon finely chopped green chilli

½ red (Spanish) onion, finely chopped

½ teaspoon turmeric

¼ teaspoon chilli powder

½–1 teaspoon salt, or to taste

30 g (1 oz) ghee (page 13) or 2 tablespoons vegetable or canola oil

lemon wedges to serve

Preheat the grill (broiler) to a medium heat or preheat the oven to 220°C (430°F).

Put the mushrooms, pepper and sesame oil in a large bowl and stir carefully to coat well. Marinate for 2 minutes.

Grill the mushrooms for 5 minutes, or cook them in the oven for 7–8 minutes.

Lightly beat the eggs in a medium bowl, then stir in the peas, coriander, green chilli, onion, turmeric, chilli powder and salt.

Heat the ghee or oil in a large frying pan over a medium heat. Pour in the egg mixture and cook, stirring gently, until scrambled, about 3 minutes. Fill each mushroom with some of the scrambled egg and serve with lemon wedges.

Alternatives: You can use this recipe as a guide for cooking other egg breakfast dishes. For example, make a masala omelette by combining the eggs with the spices and herbs. Alternatively, make eggs en cocotte with a difference – break the whole eggs into an ovenproof dish, sprinkle with the spices and herbs and bake in an oven preheated to 160°C (320°F) for 20 minutes, or until set to your liking.

Hyderabadi Kabab Nizami

Serves 4 / Makes 8–12

I first tasted this unusual recipe in a Hyderabad club known for its cutting-edge cuisine. The paté-like texture of the meat is achieved with a traditional tenderising method that uses the enzymes of kiwi fruit or unripe papaya to soften the meat. Serve these kababs as an entrée with Green Chutney (page 188) and an Onion Salad (page 180), or with wedges of flat bread or pitta bread for a shared starter.

20 g (¾ oz) Fried Onions (page 209)

2 green chillies

2 kiwi fruit, peeled and chopped, or 2 tablespoons peeled and chopped unripe papaya

500 g (1 lb 2 oz) minced (ground) lamb

1 tablespoon ginger paste (page 12)

1 teaspoon garlic paste (page 12)

juice of 1 lemon or lime

1 teaspoon garam masala (page 11)

½–1 teaspoon salt, or to taste

2 large eggs

60 g (2 oz/¼ cup) plain yoghurt

2 tablespoons saffron infusion, using 2 saffron threads only (page 13)

60 g (2 oz) ghee (page 13) or 60 ml (2 fl oz/¼ cup) vegetable or canola oil

In a food processor, blend the fried onions, chillies and kiwi fruit or papaya to form a paste.

Transfer the paste to a bowl. Add the lamb, ginger and garlic pastes, lemon or lime juice, garam masala, salt and eggs, and mix to combine well. Cover and refrigerate for 4 hours.

Mix together the yoghurt and saffron infusion in a small bowl.

Preheat the oven to 200°C (400°F). Wet your hands, then take a handful of the meat mixture and shape it into a small pyramid about 4 cm (1½ in) tall. Place on a non-stick baking tray. Repeat to use up all the mixture. Top each pyramid with 1 tablespoon of the yoghurt and saffron mixture.

Cook in the oven for 10 minutes. Baste with the ghee or oil, then return to the oven and cook for a further 7–10 minutes. Serve hot.

Beetroot and Vegetable 'chops'

Serves 4 / Makes 8–10

These crispy, breadcrumb-coated, soft, beetrooty patties have the crunch of peanuts and the firm, sweet bite of sultanas. They are a must at a Bengali wedding. Imagine the wedding guests at long tables, eating off banana leaves, the waiters bearing baskets of freshly cooked beetroot (beet) 'chops'. A chef once shared his secret ingredient for this dish with me: he used beer instead of milk for the coating! Serve as a cocktail snack or as part of an Indian meal.

1 small beetroot (beet), peeled and quartered

1 potato, peeled and quartered

2 carrots, peeled and thickly sliced

60 g (2 oz) shelled fresh or frozen peas

2 tablespoons unsalted raw peanuts

2 tablespoons sultanas (golden raisins)

1 green chilli, chopped

1 tablespoon garam masala (page 11)

½–1 teaspoon salt, or to taste

75 g (2¾ oz/½ cup) plain (all-purpose) flour

2 large eggs

125 ml (4 fl oz/½ cup) milk or beer

75 g (2¾ oz) dry or fresh breadcrumbs (see Note)

vegetable or canola oil for deep-frying

Put the beetroot in a small saucepan of boiling salted water and cook over a medium heat for 20 minutes, or until cooked through. Drain well, then roughly mash. Meanwhile, put the potato and carrot in a medium saucepan of boiling salted water and cook over a medium heat for 8 minutes. Add the peas, bring back to a boil and cook for 2 minutes. Drain well, then roughly mash.

Put the mashed beetroot, potato, carrot and peas in a large bowl. Stir in the peanuts, sultanas, chilli, garam masala and salt and mix together thoroughly. With your hands, shape the mixture into egg-shaped ovals. (You should make 8–10 with this amount of mixture.)

Put the flour on a large plate. Lightly beat the eggs with the milk or beer in a shallow bowl. Put the breadcrumbs on a separate large plate.

Roll each patty in the flour to lightly coat. Dip the floured patties in the egg and milk or beer mixture to cover completely. Allow any excess to drip off before rolling each patty in the breadcrumbs, pressing down firmly to make sure they are well coated.

Heat the oil in a wok or deep-fryer to 180°C (350°F) (see page 15). Deep-fry a few of the patties at a time for about 4 minutes, or until golden brown. Drain on kitchen towels and serve hot.

Note: Dried breadcrumbs are usually used for coating the patties, but fresh breadcrumbs give a crunchier texture.

Banana Chilli and and Potato Pakoras

Serves 4 / Makes 12

Today, India produces almost every single variety of chilli that is available globally, but chillies were in fact only introduced there in the sixteenth century. Chilli is mainly used to impart that addictive hot sensation to food, but some recipes have evolved with chilli as the star ingredient. This recipe is one of them, and despite the fact that you are biting into a chilli, these pakoras are not very hot because banana chillies are mild and also, the seeds are removed. Serve with Green Chutney (page 188) as a snack or as an accompaniment to barbecued meats.

3 potatoes, skins left on

6 banana chillies

½ teaspoon chilli powder

½ teaspoon ground amchur

½–1 teaspoon salt, or to taste

vegetable or canola oil for deep-frying

Batter

110 g (4 oz/1 cup) besan (chickpea flour)

½ teaspoon turmeric

½ teaspoon chilli powder

1 teaspoon ajwaiin seeds

½–1 teaspoon salt, or to taste

Cook the potatoes in a covered saucepan of boiling salted water over a medium heat for about 15 minutes, or until cooked through. Drain well, then leave until cool enough to handle. Peel and roughly mash. (You should have the equivalent of about 230 g (8 oz/1 cup) of mashed potato.)

While the potato is cooling, carefully cut the banana chillies in half lengthwise and remove the seeds.

Mix together the potato, chilli powder, amchur and salt in a medium bowl. Stuff each chilli half with this mixture.

To make the batter, mix together the besan, turmeric, chilli powder, ajwaiin seeds, salt and about 375 ml (12½ fl oz/1½ cups) water in a medium bowl. Add the water gradually until the batter has the correct consistency – it should coat the back of the spoon and gently drip down. (The amount of water required to achieve this consistency will depend on the type of besan you use, as some besans retain more liquid than others.)

Heat the oil in a wok or deep-fryer to 180°C (350°F) (see page 15). Carefully dip the stuffed chillies in the batter, then deep-fry them for about 5 minutes or until golden brown and crisp. Drain on kitchen towels and serve immediately.

Lentil and Prawn Wadas

Serves 4 / Makes 8

*Wadas are fried lentil or vegetable dumplings. They originate from western and southern
India and are usually served as a snack or cocktail nibble. This recipe includes prawns (shrimp),
which create an especially delicious flavour. The soft juiciness of the prawns contrasts well with
the earthy lentil flavour and crunchy texture. These wadas go well with Coconut Chutney
(page 188).*

8 raw tiger or medium prawns
(shrimp), shelled and
deveined

½ teaspoon turmeric

½–1 teaspoon salt, or to taste

115 g (4 oz) split red lentils
(masoor dal), rinsed and
drained

1 tablespoon finely chopped
onion

1 teaspoon finely chopped
green chilli

½ teaspoon chilli powder

vegetable or canola oil for
deep-frying

lime wedges to serve

Toss the prawns with the turmeric and salt in a small bowl,
then cover with plastic wrap and refrigerate.

Put the lentils in a medium bowl, cover with water and soak
for 2 hours. Drain, then transfer to a food processor and
process coarsely.

Transfer the lentil mixture to a clean bowl, add the onion,
green chilli and chilli powder and mix together. With wet
hands, shape the mixture into eight small, flat patties, about
2.5–3.5 cm (1–1½ in) in diameter (depending on the size of
the prawns). Place a prawn on top of each patty and press
down firmly.

Heat the oil in a wok or deep-fryer to a medium heat of
180°C (350°F) (see page 15). Deep-fry the patties in two
batches for about 7 minutes, or until crisp and cooked. Drain
on kitchen towels and serve hot with a fresh squeeze of lime.

Fish Amritsari

Serves 4

In busy marketplaces in the Punjab, people queue up from lunchtime to midnight to savour this aromatic freshwater fish snack, a specialty of Amritsar. Add some sliced red (Spanish) onion, a squeeze of lemon juice, wrap it all in paper and you have your fish fix for the day! These crispy fish bites are ideal for cocktail snacks or as a starter to the main meal.

500 g (1 lb 2 oz) firm white fish fillets, such as snapper, mullet, ling or cod

vegetable or canola oil for deep-frying

lemon wedges to serve

Marinade

2 tablespoons white vinegar

1 tablespoon ginger paste (page 12)

1 tablespoon garlic paste (page 12)

1 teaspoon ajwaiin seeds

1 teaspoon chilli powder

¼ teaspoon turmeric

½ teaspoon white pepper

40 g (1½ oz) besan (chickpea flour)

3–4 drops of tandoori colour (optional) (see Notes)

½–1 teaspoon salt, or to taste

Cut the fish into 2.5 cm (1 in) pieces and put in a shallow dish.

To marinate the fish, sprinkle the vinegar, ginger and garlic pastes, ajwaiin seeds, chilli powder, turmeric, white pepper, besan, tandoori colour, if using, and salt over the fish pieces and turn to coat them evenly. Cover with plastic wrap and marinate in the refrigerator for about 20 minutes.

Heat the oil in a wok or deep-fryer to 180°C (350°F) (see page 15). Deep-fry the fish, a few pieces at a time for about 7–8 minutes, or until crisp and cooked. Drain on kitchen towels and serve with lemon wedges.

Note: Sprinkling the individual marinade ingredients over the fish one after another, rather than mixing all the marinade ingredients together before coating the fish, actually results in the ingredients mixing together better and coating the fish more evenly.

Tandoori colour is an Indian food colouring that has no taste. You can buy it in Indian grocery stores.

Upma

Serves 4

Upma, meaning salt and flour, is a recipe that originates from the south of India. This is a great dish for breakfast, brunch or a light lunch. The semolina resembles a flaky, light polenta dish with the added flavour of spices, and is delicious teamed with Coconut Chutney (page 188) and Sambar Dal (page 174).

30 g (1 oz) ghee (page 13) or 2 tablespoons vegetable or canola oil

1 teaspoon black mustard seeds

1 teaspoon split white lentils (white urad dal)

½ teaspoon split yellow peas

1 teaspoon asafoetida powder

1 tablespoon curry leaves

1 tablespoon chopped onion

1 teaspoon finely chopped ginger

1 teaspoon finely chopped green chilli

½ teaspoon turmeric

125 g (4½ oz/1 cup) semolina

½–1 teaspoon salt, or to taste

1 tablespoon lemon juice

1 tablespoon finely chopped coriander (cilantro) leaves

Heat the ghee or oil in a large frying pan over a medium heat. Stir in the mustard seeds, split white lentils and split yellow peas, asafoetida powder and curry leaves, and cook until the mustard seeds start to crackle. Immediately add the onion, ginger and chilli and sauté for about 5 minutes, stirring occasionally.

Add the turmeric and semolina and stir continuously, until the semolina is well coated with the mixture. Add 250 ml (8½ fl oz/1 cup) water and the salt and cook, stirring vigorously, for 5 minutes, or until the semolina is cooked and has absorbed all the water. Stir the lemon juice and coriander through the semolina mixture and serve hot.

Onion Bhajees

Serve 4 / Makes 16

In Gujarat, pakoras, or vegetable fritters, are known as bhajees or bhajias. They are quick to cook and fun to eat as a starter or a cocktail bite. At the Spice Kitchen one of our most popular starters is named BOB (Best of British) – a combination of onion bhajees and Chicken Tikka Masala (page 123). Serve these bhajees with Tamarind and Ginger Chutney (page 186) or Lime Juice Chutney (page 196).

2 large onions, sliced

55 g (2 oz/½ cup) besan (chickpea flour)

pinch of chilli powder

pinch of turmeric

2 teaspoons white vinegar

½–1 teaspoon salt, or to taste

vegetable or canola oil for deep-frying

Mix together the onion, besan, chilli powder, turmeric, vinegar and salt in a large bowl.

Add 60–125 ml (2–4 fl oz/¼–½ cup) water to the mixture gradually, 1 tablespoon at a time, and mix together until the besan coats the onion. There should be just enough besan mixture to hold the onion slices together. (The amount of water required to achieve this consistency will depend on the type of besan you use, as some besans retain more liquid than others. Do not add too much water as the bhajees will disintegrate when fried.)

Heat the oil in a wok or deep-fryer to 180°C (350°) (see page 15). Deep-fry a few bhajees at a time for about 6–8 minutes, or until crisp and golden brown. Drain on kitchen towels and serve hot.

VEGETABLES
&
PULSES

Arguably the world's most diverse and delicious vegetarian food, the sheer variety of Indian vegetarian recipes is astounding. India has the world's largest vegetarian population, with 60–70 per cent consuming an entirely meat-free diet. As a result, wonderful dishes ranging from the simplest to the most elaborate, appear in the homes of both the rich and poor, and in restaurants throughout India. Just one or two spices are needed to enhance the distinctive flavour of individual vegetables, whether it be the humble potato, a sweet pumpkin (winter squash) or the more exotic okra.

Traditionally, vegetables and pulses are eaten together with other dishes as part of a shared Indian meal. Rice dishes such as Vegetable Biryani (page 56) and Mushroom and Chickpea Pulao (page 61) often feature alongside meat and fish dishes, as do dals, curries and simple side dishes, such as Pumpkin with Panch Phoron (page 68) or Green Bean Thoran (page 58).

Although there are many vegetarians in India, hardly any are vegan. Dairy plays an important part in Indian vegetarian cooking – yoghurt, ghee (page 13), milk, cream and panir cheese (page 13) are all used. However, for those wanting to avoid these, substitutes such as coconut milk (page 14) (for cream and milk), vinegar (for yoghurt), and ground cashews and almonds can often be used.

The dishes in this chapter can either be eaten as stand-alone meals with rice or bread or they can be part of a larger feast. Try pairing them with other recipes in this book and see which flavours you like best. There are no rules!

Spicy Pumpkin

Serves 4

As young children, we took our regular holidays in Dehradun, in the Himalayan foothills, with my grandparents. As a special treat, my grandmother would send out for this pumpkin dish with freshly made Pooris (page 204). The sight of my grandparents' cook, Moti Singh, cycling back with the goodies swinging in a bag from the handlebars would set all of us drooling, while he pretended to be affronted that we preferred the 'bought stuff' to his home-cooked delicacies. You can serve this dish as an accompaniment to meat or vegetable main courses, or by itself with pooris.

1½ tablespoons vegetable or canola oil

¼ teaspoon fennel seeds

¼ teaspoon fenugreek seeds

¼ teaspoon black mustard seeds

¼ teaspoon nigella (kalonji)

1 dried whole red chilli

500 g (1 lb 2 oz) butternut pumpkin (squash), peeled and diced

1 tablespoon tamarind pulp (page 14)

2 teaspoons sugar

1 teaspoon ground coriander

pinch of asafoetida powder

1 teaspoon chilli powder

½–1 teaspoon salt, or to taste

Heat the oil in a large saucepan over a medium heat. Add the fennel seeds, fenugreek seeds, mustard seeds, nigella, dried red chilli and pumpkin and sauté, stirring continuously to coat the pumpkin with the spices, for about 1 minute.

Stir in the tamarind pulp, sugar, coriander, asafoetida powder, chilli powder and salt with 250 ml (8½ fl oz/1 cup) water. Reduce the heat to low, cover and cook for about 30 minutes, or until the pumpkin is soft and starting to disintegrate. Serve hot.

Chickpea Masala

Serves 4

A Delhi and Punjabi street-food favourite, you can find chickpea masala and bhaturas – fluffy, fried breads – at almost every little street café and cart. The chickpea masala is arranged in a mouth-watering mound, and scattered with lemon wedges, whole green chillies, slices of red (Spanish) onion and pieces of tomato. I might never have got through university without my regular visit to the chickpea and bhatura vendor. There was always an eagerly waiting, impatient queue. Enjoy this dish as part of an Indian meal or serve with Bhaturas (page 208) for brunch or lunch.

200 g (7 oz) dried chickpeas
   or 1 × 400 g (14 oz) can
   chickpeas, rinsed and
   drained

1 black tea bag (see Note)

½–1 teaspoon salt, or to taste

1½ tablespoons vegetable or
   canola oil

1 small onion, chopped

1 tablespoon crushed garlic

1 tablespoon finely shredded
   fresh ginger

2 green chillies, slit to just
   below the stalk area, top and
   seeds left intact

1 tomato, chopped

1 tablespoon ground coriander

1 tablespoon ground cumin

pinch of turmeric

1 teaspoon chilli powder

1 teaspoon ground amchur

½ teaspoon garam masala
   (page 11)

small handful chopped
   coriander (cilantro) leaves

lemon wedges to garnish

green chillies to garnish

red (Spanish) onion quarters
   to garnish

julienned fresh ginger to
   garnish

If using dried chickpeas, soak them overnight in a large bowl of water. Drain, then put in a large saucepan with the tea bag, salt and plenty of fresh water. Cover, bring to a boil, then reduce the heat and cook over a medium heat for 1–2 hours, until tender. Skim off the residue as it rises to the surface during cooking. Drain the cooked chickpeas, reserving 250 ml (8½ fl oz/1 cup) of the cooking liquid.

Heat the oil in a large frying pan over a medium heat. Sauté the onion, stirring occasionally, for about 7 minutes, or until golden brown.

Stir in the garlic, ginger and green chillies and sauté, stirring occasionally, for 2 minutes. Add the tomato, ground coriander and cumin, turmeric, chilli powder and amchur and stir to combine, then cook for 2–3 minutes.

Stir in the cooked chickpeas and their reserved cooking liquid, or the drained canned chickpeas and 250 ml (8½ fl oz/1 cup) water. Continue cooking uncovered for 30 minutes.

When the liquid is almost absorbed, finish the dish by sprinkling in the garam masala and chopped coriander and stirring through.

Serve garnished with lemon wedges, green chillies, onion quarters and julienned ginger.

Note: The tea bag gives this dish its traditional dark colour and also a very faint tea flavour. If you use canned chickpeas, you omit the step of cooking them with the tea bag. Even so, you should still obtain a fairly good result.

Vegetable Biryani

Serves 4

Biryani is essentially a special rice dish flavoured with saffron and spices, and cooked with meat. Biryani has its origins in Persia (present-day Iran). Eleventh-century Mughals loved their rice pilafs, and these evolved into the more elaborate biryani with the addition of spices and distinctive regional ingredients. Vegetable versions are popular in India and may be served on their own, with nothing more than Boondi Raita (page 199).

60 g (2 oz) ghee (page 13) or 60 ml (2 fl oz/¼ cup) vegetable or canola oil

2 green chillies

1 teaspoon whole mace

5 cloves

5 green cardamom pods

1 teaspoon black cumin seeds (shah zeera)

1 small onion, sliced

225 g (8 oz) basmati rice or other long-grain rice, washed and drained

150 g (5½ oz/1 cup) diced mixed seasonal vegetables, choosing 4–6 of the following:

½ small eggplant (aubergine)

2 Swiss brown or field mushrooms, cleaned

2 cauliflower florets

1 carrot, peeled

40 g (1½ oz/¼ cup) frozen peas

6 green beans, trimmed

1 large potato, peeled

1 tomato

60 g (2 oz/¼ cup) plain yoghurt

1 tablespoon chopped coriander (cilantro) leaves

1 tablespoon chopped mint leaves

½–1 teaspoon salt, or to taste

1 tablespoon saffron infusion (page 13)

unsalted roasted cashew nuts to garnish

sultanas (golden raisins) to garnish

Heat the ghee or oil in a large heavy-based saucepan over a medium heat. Stir in the chillies, mace, cloves, cardamom pods and black cumin seeds and cook for 5 seconds. Immediately add the onion and sauté, stirring occasionally, for about 5 minutes, or until golden brown.

Add the rice and stir until each grain is coated with the mixture. Add the mixed vegetables of your choice and the yoghurt, coriander and mint and stir to mix through.

Stir in 625 ml (21 fl oz/2½ cups) boiling water plus the salt, then cover and cook over a high heat until it comes to a boil. Reduce the heat to low and simmer gently for about 20 minutes, or until the rice is almost cooked.

Carefully pour the saffron infusion in one place on top of the almost-cooked rice but do not stir. Cover and continue cooking for a further 15 minutes, or until all the liquid is absorbed and the vegetables are tender.

If you wish, gently stir the biryani just before serving – this is done to produce the trademark yellow and white grains of a biryani, but you must do it very carefully to avoid breaking up the rice grains. Garnish with the cashew nuts and sultanas and serve.

Green Bean Thoran

Serves 4

In the temples of South India, the temple cooks have created a style of cooking that pays attention to the physical and spiritual wellbeing of the individual. These cooks use only the best ingredients, which are donated to the temple by pilgrims. The food prepared is used as a sacrifice to the gods and is also distributed to the pilgrims, devotees of the temple and the poor. This dish is one of these temple recipes. In this particular version, the taste of coconut, curry leaves and spices adds another dimension to the sweetness of green beans. If desired, it can be served as a warm salad, accompanied by steamed basmati rice or other long-grain rice (see page 14), or Pooris (page 204) or Parathas (page 206).

1½ tablespoons vegetable or canola oil

1 whole dried red chilli

¼ teaspoon fenugreek seeds

½ teaspoon black mustard seeds

6 curry leaves

1 teaspoon ginger paste (page 12)

350 g (12½ oz) green beans, trimmed and diced

½–1 teaspoon salt, or to taste

25 g (1 oz) desiccated (grated dried) coconut or 40 g (1½ oz) freshly grated coconut

Heat the oil in a large wok or frying pan over a medium heat. Stir in the chilli, fenugreek seeds, black mustard seeds and curry leaves and cook until the mustard seeds start to crackle. Immediately add the ginger paste and beans and sauté, stirring, for about 1 minute. Stir in the salt, then reduce the heat to low, cover and cook for about 15 minutes, stirring occasionally, until the beans are tender but not overcooked.

Stir in the coconut and cook for a further 2 minutes, then serve.

Vegetable Khichadi

Serves 4

Vegetable khichadi originated as a peasant dish in ancient India. It can be cooked dry or quite wet, with vegetables or even prawns (shrimp). For me, this is the best comfort food, guaranteed to produce a warm fuzzy feeling. It is usually served for lunch, either with a spicy or sweet Tomato Chutney (page 194) or teamed with a dry meat or vegetable curry.

30 g (1 oz) ghee (page 13) or 2 tablespoons vegetable or canola oil

3 bay leaves

1 cm (½ in) cinnamon stick

3 green cardamom pods

2 black cardamom pods

4 cloves

4 black peppercorns

1 large onion, sliced

135 g (5 oz/⅔ cup) basmati rice or other long-grain rice, washed and drained

100 g (3½ oz) split dried mung beans (yellow mung dal) or split red lentils (masoor dal), washed and drained

250 g (9 oz) diced mixed seasonal vegetables, choosing 2–3 of the following:

4 small cauliflower florets

4 small new potatoes, scrubbed

1 sweet potato, peeled

12 green beans, trimmed

1 carrot, peeled

100 g (3½ oz) pumpkin (winter squash), peeled

½–1 teaspoon salt, or to taste

Heat the ghee or oil in a large heavy-based saucepan with a tight-fitting lid over a medium heat. Stir in the bay leaves, cinnamon, green and black cardamom pods, cloves and peppercorns and cook for 5 seconds. Immediately add the onion and sauté, stirring occasionally, for about 5 minutes, or until golden brown.

Add the rice and dried mung beans or lentils, the mixed vegetables of your choice, 1 litre (34 fl oz/4 cups) boiling water and the salt, and stir to mix through. Cover and bring to a boil, then reduce the heat to low and simmer for about 30–40 minutes, or until the rice and lentils are cooked. Serve hot.

Note: The consistency of khichadi may be fairly moist, like this recipe, or it may be dry. If you prefer a drier version, reduce the amount of boiling water you add with the rice, dried beans and vegetables to 625 ml (21 fl oz/2½ cups).

Mushroom and chickpea Pulao

Serves 4

There is almost less rice in this dish – another Mughal favourite – than there are other goodies. The Mughals loved their dried fruit and nuts and missed them terribly until they succeeded in growing them in India. Of course, green chillies, cashew nuts and tomatoes were probably added to this recipe later by an inventive cook. This wonderful combination is a dish in itself. Serve this pulao with a Raita (pages 198–199) and Eggplant Chutney (page 193).

60 g (2 oz) ghee (page 13) or 60 ml (2 fl oz/¼ cup) vegetable or canola oil

2 green chillies

1 teaspoon whole mace

7 cloves

7 green cardamom pods

1 teaspoon black cumin seeds (shah zeera)

1 small onion, sliced

200 g (7 oz/1 cup) basmati rice or other long-grain rice, washed and drained

4 large mushrooms, cleaned and diced

1 large tomato, diced

60 g (2 oz/¼ cup) plain yoghurt

1 tablespoon chopped coriander (cilantro) leaves

1 tablespoon chopped mint leaves

100 g (3½ oz) dried chickpeas, cooked or 160 g (5½ oz) canned chickpeas, rinsed and drained (see Note)

½–1 teaspoon salt, or to taste

1 tablespoon saffron infusion (page 13)

raw almonds to garnish

unsalted roasted cashew nuts to garnish

shelled pistachio nuts to garnish

sultanas (golden raisins) to garnish

Heat the ghee or oil in a shallow heavy-based saucepan over a medium heat. Stir in the chillies, mace, cloves, cardamom pods and black cumin seeds and cook for 5 seconds. Immediately add the onion and sauté, stirring occasionally, for about 5 minutes, or until golden brown.

Add the rice and stir until each grain is coated with the mixture. Add the mushroom, tomato, yoghurt, coriander and mint and stir to mix through.

Stir in 375 ml (12½ fl oz/1½ cups) boiling water, the chickpeas and salt. Cover and cook over a high heat until it comes to a boil. Reduce the heat to as low as possible and simmer gently for about 20 minutes, or until most of the water is absorbed and the rice is almost cooked.

Pour in the saffron infusion and stir through, then cover and continue cooking for a further 15 minutes, until all the liquid is absorbed and the vegetables are tender.

Garnish with the almonds, cashew nuts, pistachio nuts and sultanas, and serve.

Note: To cook the chickpeas, soak overnight in a large bowl of water. Drain, then put in a large saucepan with plenty of fresh water. Cover, bring to a boil, then reduce the heat to medium and cook for 1–2 hours, until tender. Skim off the residue as it rises to the surface during the cooking process. When cooked, drain the chickpeas and use according to the recipe. Alternatively, you can use canned chickpeas in this recipe. Rinse well in cold water and drain before adding them to the rice.

Corn Takatak

Serves 4

Making a takatak involves cooking at high temperatures on a hotplate or barbecue plate, and breaking up the ingredients with a metal spatula, the sound of which – 'takatak'– gives its name to the dish. This method of cooking originated in North-West India and is also well known in Pakistan, where many different ingredients, both vegetable and meat, are used. Serve this corn and tomato dish with fresh Indian bread.

15 g (½ oz) ghee (page 13), or 2 teaspoons vegetable or canola oil and 10 g (¼ oz) salted butter

pinch of ajwaiin seeds

1 tablespoon chopped onion

1 teaspoon chopped fresh ginger

250 g (9 oz/1 cup) tomato purée (puréed tomatoes) or 3 tomatoes, skin and seeds removed, puréed (see Note)

1 tablespoon tomato paste (concentrated purée)

1 teaspoon ground coriander

1 teaspoon dried fenugreek leaves

½ teaspoon chilli powder

½–1 teaspoon salt, or to taste

200 g (7 oz/1 cup) corn kernels cut from the cob

2 tablespoons chopped coriander (cilantro) leaves

Heat the ghee or oil and butter in a large heavy-based frying pan or on a barbecue hotplate over a high heat. Add the ajwaiin seeds, then immediately add the onion and sauté, stirring frequently, for about 2 minutes, or until light brown. Stir in the ginger and sauté for 1 minute.

Add the tomato purée, tomato paste, ground coriander, fenugreek leaves, chilli powder and salt and cook for about 1 minute, stirring continuously.

Stir in the corn, reduce the heat to low and simmer for about 5 minutes, until tender. Scatter over the chopped coriander and serve hot.

Note: *If you are using whole tomatoes to make the tomato purée, score a cross in the base of each tomato. Put in a heatproof bowl and cover with boiling water. Leave for 30 seconds, then transfer to cold water. When cool enough to handle, peel the skin away, starting from the cross. Cut the tomato in half crosswise, scoop out the seeds with a teaspoon and discard. Process the tomato flesh in a food processor to form a purée.*

Kum Kum Tamatar

Serves 4

With over 60 per cent of the population classified as vegetarian in India, there is no end of exciting vegetarian recipes that are special dishes in themselves, and not just a substitute for meat. An innovative and delicious recipe for special occasions, kum kum tamatar is a unique dish, and very popular at the Spice Kitchen. One of our guests even cooks it in his wood-fired oven and swears by the resulting smoky flavours of the eggplant and tomato combination. You can serve this dish on its own with Naan (page 200) or Pooris (page 204), or as part of an Indian feast.

1 eggplant (aubergine)

4 large or 8 medium vine-ripened or ripe tomatoes

1 tablespoon mustard oil

1 tablespoon finely chopped onion

1 teaspoon ginger paste (page 12)

1 teaspoon garlic paste (page 12)

1 tablespoon finely chopped green chilli

1 tablespoon finely chopped coriander (cilantro) leaves

½ teaspoon turmeric

½–1 teaspoon salt, or to taste

coriander (cilantro) leaves to garnish

Rogini Sauce

60 g (2 oz) ghee (page 13) or 60 ml (2 fl oz/¼ cup) vegetable or canola oil

½ teaspoon ginger paste (page 12)

½ teaspoon garlic paste (page 12)

1 teaspoon ground coriander

½ teaspoon turmeric

½ teaspoon chilli powder

40 g (1½ oz/¼ cup) raw cashew nuts

1 onion, sliced

190 ml (6½ fl oz/¾ cup) thick (double/heavy) cream

2 tablespoons tomato paste (concentrated purée)

¼ teaspoon saffron infusion (page 13)

3–4 drops of kewra essence (see Note)

½–1 teaspoon salt, or to taste

To make the rogini sauce, heat the ghee or oil in a large frying pan over a medium heat. Sauté the ginger and garlic pastes for about 30 seconds. Add the ground coriander, turmeric, chilli powder, cashew nuts, onion, cream and tomato paste with 250 ml (8½ fl oz/1 cup) water. Stir to combine and heat through, then reduce the heat to low and simmer gently for 20 minutes. Allow the mixture to cool a little, then purée in a food processor.

Meanwhile, roast the eggplant in a heavy-based frying pan or chargrill pan over a medium heat, or under the grill (broiler), for about 20 minutes, or until soft and the skin is charred. Turn the eggplant only once or twice during cooking. Leave until it is cool enough to handle, then cut the eggplant in half. Scoop out the flesh with a spoon, chop roughly and set aside. Discard the skin.

Cut the tops off the tomatoes and discard. Scoop out the juice and flesh with a spoon, leaving just the hollowed-out shells of the tomatoes. Reserve the flesh and the shells separately.

Heat the mustard oil in a separate frying pan over a medium heat. Sauté the onion, stirring occasionally, for about 3 minutes, or until golden brown. Add the ginger and garlic pastes and cook, stirring, for 1 minute. Add the chilli, chopped coriander, turmeric, reserved eggplant and tomato flesh and salt. Stir to mix well, then cover and cook for 5 minutes. Remove from the heat.

Using a spoon, fill the hollowed-out tomatoes with the tomato and eggplant mixture, pressing it in firmly.

Return the puréed rogini sauce to the frying pan and heat through over a low heat. Add the saffron infusion, kewra essence and salt and stir through.

Carefully put the stuffed tomatoes in the sauce and simmer gently over a low heat for about 20 minutes, until they are soft.

Garnish with coriander leaves and serve hot.

Note: Kewra essence is extracted from the keora flower and is used to flavour rich Mughal curries and rice dishes. The essence is concentrated and should be used sparingly. You can purchase it in Asian and Indian grocery stores.

Sweet Potato and Turnip Bhurta

Serves 4

Vegetable recipes in India are never boring. There are endless combinations of spices and cooking techniques, which vary from region to region. Even the meat eaters must have two or three vegetable dishes as part of their meal. This recipe is a very satisfying comfort food that can be eaten with anything. A bhurta is a rough mash, found in the north and east of India. It describes a special home-style method of cooking vegetables such as potatoes, eggplants (aubergines) and turnips. Serve this dish as an accompaniment to meat or fish dishes or as part of a vegetarian meal.

2 large sweet potatoes, peeled and cut into 3 cm (1¼ in) pieces

2 turnips, peeled and cut into 3 cm (1¼ in) pieces

1 teaspoon vegetable or canola oil (optional)

15 g (½ oz) ghee (page 13) or 1 tablespoon vegetable or canola oil

1 dried whole red chilli

½ teaspoon fenugreek seeds

1 small onion, chopped

2 green chillies, seeds removed to reduce heat if desired, chopped

2 tomatoes, chopped

2 tablespoons chopped coriander (cilantro) leaves

1 teaspoon turmeric

½–1 teaspoon salt, or to taste

Place the sweet potato and turnip in a saucepan of boiling salted water and cook for 10 minutes, until tender. Alternatively, put in a roasting tin, toss with the 1 teaspoon vegetable or canola oil and roast in an oven preheated to 180°C (350°F) for 20 minutes, or until tender. Roughly mash the sweet potato and turnip and set aside.

Heat the ghee or oil in a large frying pan over a medium heat. Stir in the dried red chilli and fenugreek seeds and cook for 5 seconds. Immediately add the onion and sauté, stirring occasionally, for about 5 minutes, or until golden brown.

Add the sweet potato and turnip mash, green chilli, tomato, coriander, turmeric and salt. Stir well to combine, then reduce the heat to low and cook gently, stirring frequently, for 5 minutes. Serve hot.

Tomatoes Filled with Mushrooms and Figs

Serves 4

When tomatoes are in season, this is a great dish to make for a dinner party. Indians love stuffed vegetable recipes for a vegetarian dish with a difference. We use eggplant (aubergine), capsicum (pepper), zucchini (courgette), potato, okra, bitter melon (bitter gourd), even between the stalks and florets of broccoli, for filling with various ingredients, such as panir or cheddar cheese, sultanas (golden raisins), nuts, tamarind, dried fruit, coconut or even meat. Serve these stuffed tomatoes with just about any of the Indian breads.

8 ripe tomatoes

60 ml (2 fl oz/¼ cup) vegetable or canola oil

1 onion, chopped

1 teaspoon ginger paste (page 12)

1 teaspoon garlic paste (page 12)

1 teaspoon ground coriander

½ teaspoon turmeric

1 teaspoon chilli powder

2 tablespoons plain yoghurt

½–1 teaspoon salt, or to taste

125 ml (4 fl oz/½ cup) pouring (single/light) cream

¼ teaspoon freshly ground whole mace

¼ teaspoon ground cardamom

Filling

1 teaspoon vegetable or canola oil

100–150 g (3½–5½ oz) mushrooms, cleaned and finely chopped

1 teaspoon finely chopped green chilli

1 teaspoon finely chopped ginger

125 g (4½ oz) fresh figs or 50–75 g (1¾–2¾ oz) dried figs, finely chopped

½–1 teaspoon salt, or to taste

Cut the tops off the tomatoes and discard. Scoop out the juice and flesh with a spoon, leaving the hollowed-out shells of the tomatoes. Reserve the flesh and the shells separately.

To make the filling, heat the oil in a medium frying pan or saucepan over a medium heat. Sauté the mushrooms, chilli and ginger, stirring occasionally, for about 5 minutes. Add the figs and salt and cook, stirring occasionally, for about 10 minutes if using fresh figs, or for 6 minutes if using dried figs.

Using a spoon, fill the hollowed-out tomatoes with the filling, pressing it in firmly. Set aside.

In a large frying pan, heat the oil over a low heat. Sauté the onion, stirring occasionally, for about 5 minutes, or until golden brown. Stir in the ginger and garlic pastes and cook for 2 minutes. Add the coriander, turmeric, chilli powder, reserved tomato flesh, yoghurt and salt and stir, then cook until heated through. Stir in the cream and simmer for 2 minutes. Combine the mace and cardamom in a small bowl, then stir into the sauce.

Carefully place the stuffed tomatoes in the sauce and simmer gently over a low heat for about 20 minutes, or until they are soft. (You can cover the pan if you want to speed up the cooking time.) Serve hot.

Pumpkin with Panch Phoron

Serves 4

Bengal is the only region in India where food is traditionally served in a succession of courses. First, vegetables are served with steamed rice, followed by dal, fish and meat curries. This dish of pumpkin with panch phoron is a typical Bengali recipe – a simply cooked vegetable with the five spices found in panch phoron highlighting the vegetable's natural flavours. Serve with other curries and steamed rice (see page 14).

1 tablespoon mustard oil

1 dried whole red chilli

1 teaspoon panch phoron (page 12)

500 g (1 lb 2 oz) pumpkin (winter squash), such as butternut, jap or kent, peeled and diced

½ teaspoon sugar (optional)

½–1 teaspoon salt, or to taste

Heat the mustard oil in a small wok or frying pan over a medium heat. Stir in the chilli and panch phoron and cook until the panch phoron starts to crackle.

Immediately stir in the pumpkin, sugar, if using, and salt. Add 125 ml (4 fl oz/½ cup) water, then reduce the heat to low, cover and cook, stirring occasionally, for about 30 minutes, or until the pumpkin is soft. Serve hot.

Karahi-style Baby Spinach and Mushrooms

Serves 4

Karahi-style cooking is done over a high heat for a very short period of time. The extreme heat leads to its characteristic flavour. A karahi is an Indian wok that is slightly deeper than a traditional Asian wok and made of a thicker metal, such as cast iron. It is used for stir-frying, deep-frying and simmering, covered, over a very low heat to preserve colour and flavour. Serve this karahi of spinach and mushrooms with Naan (page 200), Bhaturas (page 208) or Parathas (page 206).

80 g (2¾ oz) ghee (page 13) or 80 ml (3 fl oz/⅓ cup) vegetable or canola oil

2 tablespoons garlic paste (page 12)

4 tablespoons balti masala (page 12)

5 tomatoes, chopped

3 green chillies, chopped

2 tablespoons finely chopped fresh ginger

large handful coriander (cilantro) leaves, chopped

180 g (6½ oz) large mushrooms, cleaned and diced, or button mushrooms, cleaned

125 g (4½ oz) baby spinach, washed and drained

½–1 teaspoon salt, or to taste

Heat the ghee or oil in a wok or large frying pan over a high heat. Stir-fry the garlic paste for 2 minutes, or until golden brown. Add the balti masala and stir-fry for 1 minute.

Stir in the tomato and cook until it starts to bubble. Add the chilli, three-quarters of the ginger and one-third of the coriander leaves, stir to mix well and simmer for 5 minutes.

Stir in the mushrooms and baby spinach and cook for about 3 minutes, or until tender. Season with the salt to taste and stir well.

Garnish with the remaining ginger and coriander leaves and serve hot.

Mixed Vegetable Navratan Curry

Serves 4

This dish takes its name from the nine famous wise men of Akbar's Mughal court in fourteenth-century Agra. Navratan literally means 'nine gems', and many dishes, which usually comprised nine ingredients, were named after these nine wise courtiers. This recipe is an easy, everyday vegetable curry with great flavours and textures, using both root and green vegetables. Serve it as a vegetarian main course or as part of an Indian meal with Pulao Rice (page 167) or fresh Pooris (page 204), Parathas (page 206) or Chapattis (page 202).

1 tablespoon ground cumin

1 tablespoon ground coriander

1 teaspoon turmeric

1 teaspoon chilli powder

2 tablespoons vegetable or canola oil

1 small potato, peeled and diced

½ small sweet potato, peeled and diced

1 small carrot, peeled and diced

1 small turnip, peeled and diced

150 g (5½ oz) pumpkin (winter squash), peeled and diced

2 cauliflower florets, each cut lengthwise into 8 pieces

100 g (3½ oz) shredded cabbage

6 green beans, trimmed and diced

40 g (1½ oz/¼ cup) shelled fresh or frozen peas

125 g (4½ oz/½ cup) tomato paste (concentrated purée)

½–1 teaspoon salt, or to taste

coriander (cilantro) leaves to garnish

Mix the ground cumin and coriander, turmeric and chilli powder together with 60 ml (2 fl oz/¼ cup) water in a small bowl to make a paste.

Heat the oil in a large saucepan over a medium heat. Stir in the spice paste and cook for 5–10 seconds.

Add the potato, sweet potato, carrot and turnip with 375 ml (12½ fl oz/1½ cups) water, and stir to mix through. Cover and cook over a medium heat for 25 minutes, or until the vegetables are three-quarters cooked.

Add the pumpkin, cauliflower, cabbage, beans, peas and tomato paste, and stir to mix through. Reduce the heat to low, cover and cook for a further 15 minutes. Add salt to taste just before serving.

Garnish with the coriander leaves and serve hot.

Note: The total amount of vegetables used in this recipe should come to about 300 g (10½ oz/2 cups), once you've done all the peeling, dicing, and shredding.

Vegetable Chakka

Serves 4

A Bengali favourite with slightly sweet overtones, this simple dish uses six different vegetables that complement each other in taste and texture. 'Chakka' means six ingredients tossed together quickly. Make sure the vegetables are in their prime, preferably organic and in season, as in this recipe there is nowhere for them to hide. The whole spices accentuate the pure fresh flavours of the vegetables. Serve with steamed rice (see page 14).

1½ tablespoons mustard oil

1 teaspoon panch phoron (page 12)

2 dried whole red chillies

2 bay leaves

2.5 cm (1 in) cinnamon stick

2 cloves

1 teaspoon ginger paste (page 12)

1 small eggplant (aubergine), cut into 2.5 cm (1 in) pieces

200 g (7 oz) pumpkin (winter squash), peeled and cut into 2.5 cm (1 in) pieces

1 sweet potato, peeled and cut into 2.5 cm (1 in) pieces

1 zucchini (courgette), thickly sliced

4 cauliflower florets, each cut lengthwise into 4 pieces

12 green beans, trimmed and sliced into 2.5 cm (1 in) lengths

1 teaspoon sugar

1 teaspoon turmeric

½–1 teaspoon salt, or to taste

Heat the mustard oil in a wok or large frying pan over a medium heat. Stir in the panch phoron and chillies and cook until the mixture crackles. Immediately add the bay leaves, cinnamon, cloves and ginger paste and cook, stirring continuously, for 1 minute.

Add the eggplant, pumpkin, sweet potato, zucchini, cauliflower, beans, sugar, turmeric and salt. Stir to mix well, then cover with a tight-fitting lid and cook over the lowest heat possible for about 30 minutes or until the vegetables are tender. Only take the lid off to check and stir once during the cooking time. (This dish obtains the best taste when the vegetables cook in their own steam, without the addition of water. This can only be achieved when the lowest possible heat is used and when the lid is not opened more than once during cooking.) Serve hot.

Note: *All the vegetables should be cut to the same size as much as possible. The prepared vegetables should come to about 600 g (1 lb 5 oz) in total before cooking.*

Spinach with Panir Cheese

Serves 4

On offer in almost every Indian restaurant, this North Indian combination of spinach and panir cheese is easy to make at home. If you have never made panir cheese before, do have a go and savour the feeling of accomplishment – and the taste – you get from making your first cheese. English spinach will give the best flavour and texture to this dish, but you can use silverbeet (Swiss chard) if necessary. Serve hot with Naan (page 200), Parathas (page 206) or Chapattis (page 202).

1 teaspoon vegetable or canola oil

1 small onion, chopped

1 teaspoon chopped fresh ginger

1 teaspoon chopped garlic

1 green chilli, chopped

1 teaspoon ground coriander

½ teaspoon turmeric

240 g (8½ oz) English spinach, washed, drained and chopped

1 teaspoon dried fenugreek leaves

250 g (9 oz) panir cheese (page 13), diced

Heat the oil in a large saucepan over a medium heat. Sauté the onion, stirring occasionally, for about 5–7 minutes, or until light brown.

Stir in the ginger, garlic and chilli and cook for 1 minute. Add the coriander, turmeric, spinach and fenugreek leaves and cook, stirring occasionally, for about 2 minutes, or until the spinach is just done.

Remove from the heat and allow to cool, then process in a food processor to form a purée.

Return the puréed spinach mixture to the pan. Add the panir cheese and stir through the spinach. Heat gently over a low heat until hot, then serve.

Egg and Potato Curry

Serves 4

I love eggs in any form and this whole egg recipe never fails to deliver. There are always times when there is no meat or fish at home, lunch or dinner has to be on the table in 30 minutes, or 'friends for drinks' become 'friends staying on for dinner'! There is no need to panic because that wonderful versatile and delicious ingredient, the egg, is at hand. Serve this curry with steamed rice (see page 14) and Chapattis (page 202) or Parathas (page 206).

60 ml (2 fl oz/¼ cup) vegetable or canola oil

8 hard-boiled eggs, peeled

4 green cardamom pods

4 cloves

1 large onion, chopped

1 teaspoon chilli powder

1 teaspoon turmeric

1 tablespoon ground coriander

1 tablespoon ground cumin

1 tablespoon ginger paste (page 12)

1 tablespoon garlic paste (page 12)

2 tomatoes, chopped, or 60 g (2 oz/¼ cup) tomato paste (concentrated purée)

½–1 teaspoon salt, or to taste

8 small new potatoes, scrubbed clean and halved

chopped coriander (cilantro) leaves to garnish

Heat the oil in a large saucepan over a high heat. Sauté the hard-boiled eggs, stirring continuously, for about 4 minutes, or until they form a golden skin on the outside. Remove the eggs from the saucepan and set aside.

In the same saucepan, stir in the cardamom pods and cloves and cook over a medium heat for 5 seconds. Immediately add the onion and sauté, stirring occasionally, for about 7 minutes, or until golden brown.

Meanwhile, mix the chilli powder, turmeric, ground coriander and cumin together with 60 ml (2 fl oz/¼ cup) water in a small bowl to make a paste.

Add the ginger and garlic pastes to the onion in the saucepan and cook, stirring, for about 1 minute. Add the spice paste and cook, stirring, for about 1 minute, or until the oil separates from the spices. Add the chopped tomato or tomato paste with 250 ml (8½ fl oz/1 cup) water and stir to mix through. Stir in the salt and potatoes. Reduce the heat to low, cover and cook for 25 minutes, or until the potatoes are three-quarters cooked.

Add the reserved eggs with 60 ml (2 fl oz/¼ cup) water and stir through carefully. Reduce the heat to low, cover and cook for a further 7 minutes.

Garnish with the chopped coriander and serve hot.

Green Peas with Ginger and Lemon

Serves 4

As a child, I loved helping my extended family shell the peas to make this simple, fresh and delicious recipe. Many winter afternoons in Delhi were spent sitting in the warmth of the sun with a huge stack of fresh peas, discussing the really important issues of life, such as what should accompany the green peas at dinner! To do justice to the delicate flavours of this dish, you should really use fresh peas. You can use frozen peas, but the results will not be as good. Also, eat it on its own so you can taste every element.

310 g (11 oz) shelled fresh or frozen peas

15 g (½ oz) ghee (page 13) or salted butter

1 green chilli

1 teaspoon ginger paste (page 12)

½ teaspoon sugar

1 tablespoon lemon juice

½–1 teaspoon salt, or to taste

Cook the peas in a large saucepan of boiling salted water over a high heat for 2–3 minutes, or until just tender. Drain and rinse under cold water.

Heat the ghee or butter in a large frying pan over a medium heat. Sauté the chilli and ginger paste, stirring continuously, for about 30 seconds. Stir in the peas and sugar and cook, stirring occasionally, for 2–4 minutes, or until heated through and the sugar has dissolved.

Quickly toss the lemon juice and salt through the peas, then serve.

Smoky Eggplant Bhurta

Serves 4

In this North Indian delicacy, roasted eggplant (aubergine) is the star. There are many varieties of eggplant, but this recipe is best made with the medium-sized round or long purple varieties. For the best flavour and texture, buy eggplants when they are in season and opt for the smaller, seedless ones that feel heavy for their size. Enjoy this dish hot, with Chapattis (page 202) or Parathas (page 206).

2 eggplants (aubergines)

1½ tablespoons vegetable or canola oil

1 small onion, chopped

1 teaspoon ginger paste (page 12)

1 teaspoon garlic paste (page 12)

2 large tomatoes, chopped

2 green chillies, chopped

½ teaspoon turmeric

large handful coriander (cilantro) leaves, chopped

½–1 teaspoon salt, or to taste

Roast the eggplants whole in a heavy-based frying pan or chargrill pan over a medium heat, or under the grill (broiler), for about 20 minutes, or until soft and the skin is charred. Turn only once or twice during cooking. Allow to cool, then cut in half. Scoop out the flesh with a spoon, chop roughly and reserve. Discard the skin.

Heat the oil in a frying pan over a medium heat. Sauté the onion, stirring occasionally, for 5 minutes, until translucent. Add the ginger and garlic pastes and cook, stirring, for about 1 minute.

Stir in the tomato, chilli and turmeric, reduce the heat to low and cook for about 5 minutes, or until the tomato has softened.

Stir in the reserved eggplant flesh, coriander and salt and cook for a further 5 minutes. Serve hot.

Okra Do Pyaz

Serves 4

Okra, or lady's fingers as they are known in India, is a summer vegetable, best eaten when in season, and a favourite vegetable of mine. Use only young okra and cook them uncovered to acheive a crisp – as opposed to a slimy – texture. While frozen okra is available from Indian and Middle Eastern grocery stores, it lacks the crisp texture and flavour of fresh okra. In this dish the okra is cooked with tomato and onion – do pyaz means 'double onion'. Serve it as an accompaniment to a main meal.

2 tablespooons vegetable or canola oil

1 teaspoon cumin seeds

1 dried whole red chilli

1 onion, sliced

250 g (9 oz) small, young okra

2 tomatoes, cut into wedges

½ teaspoon turmeric

½–1 teaspoon salt, or to taste

Heat the oil in a large wok or frying pan over a medium heat. Stir in the cumin seeds and chilli and cook until the cumin seeds start to crackle. Immediately add the onion and sauté, stirring occasionally, for about 5 minutes, or until translucent.

Add the okra, tomato and turmeric, stir to mix through, then cook uncovered for 15 minutes, or until the okra is soft.

Add the salt and cook for a further 2–3 minutes. (It is important to add the salt last; otherwise the okra has a tendency to become slimy.) Serve hot.

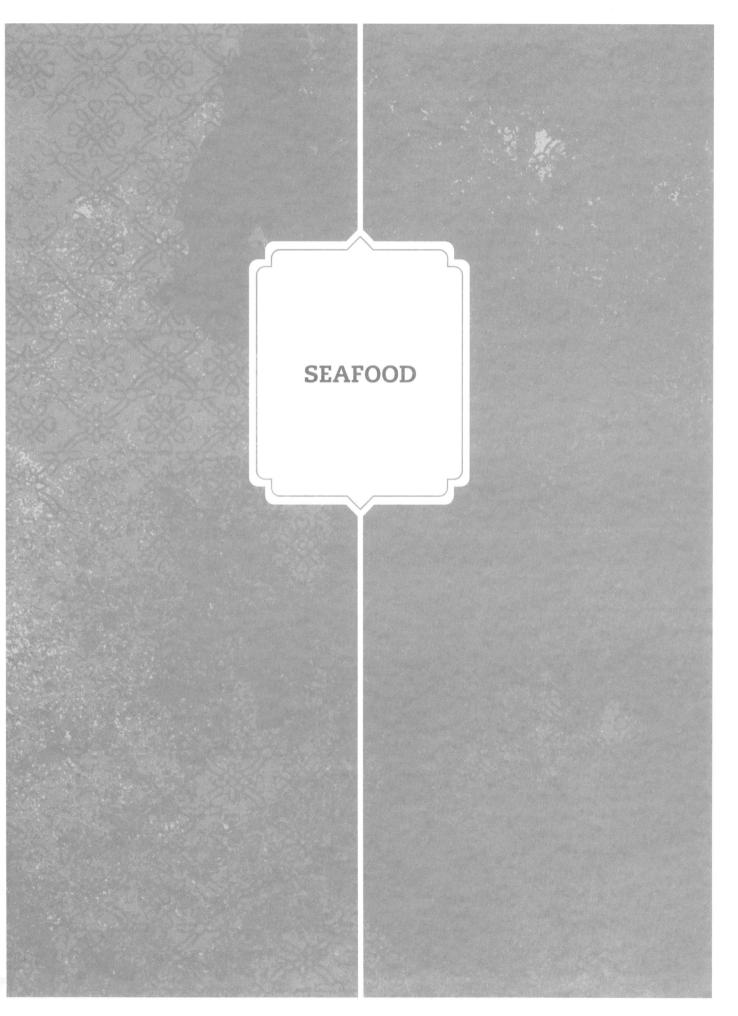

SEAFOOD

To many people, Indian food is not normally associated with seafood, as the most popular exported dishes usually contain chicken or lamb. However, the Indian subcontinent is bordered by sea on three sides: the Arabian Sea to the west, the Indian Ocean to the south and the Bay of Bengal to the east, and all are full of delectable local fish.

Moreover, there is an entire intricate network of major rivers running across the length and breadth of the country supplying towns and villages with freshwater seafood. The famous Ganges River originates in the Himalayas and flows down through India, joined by many tributaries, all full of exotic river fish such as trout, elish (local salmon) bhetki (similar to barramundi), pomfret and the much-loved rui or rohu (similar to trevally). These fish, along with coastal shellfish, supply India with a diverse repertoire of seafood recipes that can range from fried or barbecued fish, such as Tandoori Fish Tikkas (page 88), cooked shellfish, such as Crab Malabar (page 102) or Scampi Kerala Curry (page 100), to simple fish curries, such as Bengal Tomato Fish Jhal (page 86).

In many parts of India no ceremonial meal would be complete without seafood, and some of these dishes feature in this chapter. You can serve these recipes on their own or as part of a larger Indian feast. They are easy to prepare and filled with delicate flavours.

Bengal Tomato Fish Jhal

Serves 4

If you cook only one fish recipe from this book, this should be the one – a delicious, tomatoey, hot fish curry with the bold flavours of panch phoron. Once tasted, you will be immediately transported to the sights and smells of India. Serve this dish with steamed basmati rice (see page 14).

1 kg (2 lb 3 oz) firm white fish fillets, such as snapper, mulloway, ling, cod or kingfish, cut into 5 cm (2 in) pieces

2 teaspoons turmeric

1–2 teaspoons salt, or to taste

100 ml (3½ fl oz) vegetable or canola oil

2 dried whole red chillies

1 teaspoon panch phoron (page 12)

1 tablespoon ginger paste (page 12)

1 tablespoon garlic paste (page 12)

½ teaspoon chilli powder

2 green chillies, slit to just below the stalk area, top and seeds left intact

2 tablespoons tomato paste (concentrated purée)

1 tomato, chopped

coriander (cilantro) leaves to garnish

Put the fish in a large bowl. Sprinkle with 1 teaspoon of the turmeric and ½–1 teaspoon of the salt and toss together until the fish pieces are well coated.

Heat the oil in a large frying pan over a high heat. Fry the fish pieces for about 1 minute on each side just to seal them – do not cook through. Transfer to a plate and set aside.

In the same oil, add the dried red chillies and panch phoron and cook until the mixture crackles. Immediately add the ginger and garlic pastes, the remaining turmeric, the chilli powder and green chillies and stir-fry for 1 minute. Stir in the tomato paste, chopped tomato and remaining salt if desired, and cook for 2 minutes.

Stir in 125 ml (4 fl oz/½ cup) water and bring the mixture to a boil, then reduce the heat to low and simmer for 10 minutes.

Return the fish to the pan, stir gently through the sauce and then cook for a further 5 minutes.

Garnish with the coriander and serve hot.

'Doi Maach' - Fish Yoghurt Curry

Serves 4

Bengal is famous for its fish and seafood recipes. In fact in Bengal, Brahmins – the priestly class, who are normally vegetarian – are allowed to eat seafood as it is classified as a 'vegetable of the sea'! Doi maach means 'yoghurt fish'. Whole small fish or fillets can all be used and no part of the fish is wasted – fish heads are a delicacy. This recipe is my daughter's favourite – minimum effort, maximum impression. Serve it with steamed basmati rice (see page 14).

1 kg (2 lb 3 oz) fish fillets, such as snapper, mullet, bream, perch, kingfish, barramundi, ling or cod, skin left on, cut into 7.5 cm (3 in) pieces

3 teaspoons turmeric

1½–2 teaspoons salt, or to taste

150 ml (5 fl oz) mustard oil or other vegetable oil

1 large onion, chopped

2 teaspoons ginger paste (page 12)

2 teaspoons garlic paste (page 12)

1 teaspoon chilli powder

2 teaspoons sugar

125 g (4½ oz/½ cup) plain yoghurt

30 g (1 oz/¼ cup) sultanas (golden raisins)

4 green cardamom pods, roasted and ground (page 10) (see Note)

5 cloves, roasted and ground (page 10) (see Note)

1 cm (½ in) cinnamon stick, roasted and ground (page 10) (see Note)

Put the fish in a large bowl. Sprinkle with 1½ teaspoons of the turmeric and 1 teaspoon of the salt and toss together until the fish pieces are well coated.

Heat the oil in a wok or large frying pan over a medium heat. If you are using mustard oil, heat it until it is smoking. Cook the fish for 2 minutes on each side. Remove from the wok and set aside.

In the same oil, sauté the onion, stirring occasionally, for about 4 minutes or until golden brown. Add the ginger and garlic pastes, the remaining turmeric and salt, and chilli powder. Cook, stirring, over a medium heat for 2 minutes. Add the sugar and continue stirring until it dissolves.

Stir in the yoghurt and sultanas. The resulting sauce should have the consistency of a thick soup. Add up to 125 ml (4 fl oz/½ cup) water if necessary to obtain this consistency. (Some yoghurts have a runnier consistency than others.) Reduce the heat to low, cover and simmer for 15 minutes.

Return the fish to the wok, stir gently through the sauce and then sprinkle with 2 teaspoons of the combined cardamom, clove and cinnamon spice mix. Simmer for a further 10 minutes. Serve hot.

Note: Roast and grind the cardamom pods, cloves and cinnamon together. This should give you 2 teaspoons of roasted and ground spice mix.

Tandoori Fish Tikkas

Serves 4

Barbecued or grilled (broiled) dishes form a major part of Indian cooking and use the tandoor or sigri (a charcoal fire). At home, a barbecue will help you obtain the traditional smoky flavour, or you can use a chargrill pan or a conventional oven. This method of cooking is especially suited to fish and is fast, healthy and easy. Just be careful not to overcook the fish as it can become dry, leathery and unappetising if cooked for too long. Serve this dish with Green Chutney (page 188), lemon wedges and Onion Salad (page 180).

800 g (1 lb 12 oz) firm fish fillets, such as snapper, kingfish, ocean trout, salmon, mulloway, barramundi, tuna, ling or cod, cut into 3 cm (1¼ in) pieces

lemon wedges to garnish

Marinade
250 g (9 oz/1 cup) plain yoghurt

1 tablespoon mustard oil

1 tablespoon lime or lemon juice

1 teaspoon ginger paste (page 12)

1 teaspoon garlic paste (page 12)

1 teaspoon garam masala (page 11)

1 teaspoon ajwaiin seeds

1 teaspoon chilli powder

1 teaspoon turmeric

½–1 teaspoon salt, or to taste

2 tablespoons besan (chickpea flour)

1 egg, beaten

To make the marinade, put the yoghurt in the middle of a clean square of muslin (cheesecloth) resting in a bowl or container. Bring the corners in to meet at the centre and tie in a knot. Hang the bundle containing the yoghurt from a hook, place the container underneath to catch the whey and excess liquid, and leave to drain for 2 hours. In warmer weather, hang the bundle in the refrigerator.

When the yoghurt has drained, continue making the marinade. Transfer the yoghurt to a large bowl. Mix together with the mustard oil, lime or lemon juice, ginger and garlic pastes, garam masala, ajwaiin seeds, chilli powder, turmeric, salt, besan and egg.

Add the fish pieces to the marinade and stir to coat well, then cover and put in the refrigerator to marinate for up to 20 minutes – do not leave it for longer, as the fish will start to 'cook' in the acidity of the lime or lemon juice.

Meanwhile, preheat the barbecue, grill (broiler) or chargrill pan to medium–hot. Alternatively, preheat the oven to 200°C (400°F).

Thread the fish pieces onto metal skewers.

If using a grill or oven, arrange the skewers on a baking tray. Cook under the grill or in the oven for about 5–7 minutes, or until the fish is just cooked through, turning once. Alternatively, arrange the skewers on the barbecue or chargrill pan and cook for about 5–7 minutes, or until cooked, turning once.

Garnish with the lemon wedges and serve hot.

Twice-cooked Fish Jhalferazie

Serves 4

Kolkata (Calcutta) took centre stage in the establishment of British power in India. Alongside the introduction of bureaucratic systems, Western literature and music, an interesting mix of Anglo-Indian food developed. The colonial British came up with a unique dish called the 'jhalferazie' – jhal means 'hot' and ferazie apparently refers to a 'fry up'. Usually cooked with left-over roast meat, this fish version is my own twist on the recipe. It is perfect with steamed basmati rice (see page 14).

800 g (1 lb 12 oz) firm white fish fillets, such as snapper, morwong (deep sea bream), perch, mulloway, ling, cod or other meaty fish, cut into 1 x 3 cm (½ x 1¼ in) pieces

100 ml (3½ fl oz) vegetable or canola oil for shallow-frying

Marinade

1 teaspoon chopped fresh ginger

1 teaspoon chopped garlic

1 tablespoon chopped onion

1 teaspoon chilli powder

2 green chillies

1 teaspoon turmeric

½–1 teaspoon salt, or to taste

small handful coriander (cilantro) leaves, chopped

1 tablespoon white vinegar

1 tablespoon besan (chickpea flour)

Jhalferazie Sauce

1 tablespoon mustard oil

1 green chilli, slit to just below the stalk area, seeds left in

½ teaspoon cumin seeds

1 onion, sliced

125 g (4½ oz/½ cup) tomato purée (puréed tomatoes) or 2 tomatoes, skin and seeds removed, puréed (see Note)

½ green capsicum (pepper), sliced

½ red capsicum (pepper), sliced

1 teaspoon finely shredded fresh ginger

½–1 teaspoon salt, or to taste

To make the marinade, put the ginger, garlic, onion, chilli powder, green chillies, turmeric, salt, coriander and vinegar in a food processor and blend until smooth.

Put the fish in a large bowl, add the marinade and stir to coat the fish thoroughly. Stir in the besan, then cover and put in the refrigerator to marinate for 20 minutes.

Heat the vegetable oil in a large frying pan over a medium heat. Shallow-fry the fish for about 3 minutes on each side or until cooked. This will depend on the type and thickness of the fish. Once the fish flakes easily when pressed, it is ready. Remove from the pan, drain on kitchen towels and set aside.

To make the jhalferazie sauce, heat the mustard oil in a large frying pan over a high heat. When the oil is smoking, stir in the green chilli and cumin seeds, then immediately add the onion and sauté for 3 minutes, stirring occasionally. Stir in the tomato purée, green and red capsicum, ginger, salt and 125 ml (4 fl oz/½ cup) water. Bring to a boil, then reduce the heat to low and simmer for 5 minutes. Add the fried fish and carefully stir through the sauce until heated through, then serve hot.

Note: If you are using whole tomatoes to make the tomato purée, score a cross in the base of each tomato. Put in a heatproof bowl and cover with boiling water. Leave for 30 seconds, then transfer to cold water. When cool enough to handle, peel the skin away, starting from the cross. Cut the tomato in half, scoop out the seeds with a teaspoon and discard. Process the tomato flesh in a food processor to form a purée.

Bengal Fish Charchori

Serves 4

In Bengal, there are almost as many fish recipes as there are fish eaters (and almost everyone in the state eats fish). In my restaurant, this dish was one of the early favourites, a signature recipe that distinguished the Spice Kitchen from the ubiquitous 'fish everyway' served in other Indian restaurants. Charchori has come to refer to a cooking method where various ingredients are cooked together until each ingredient is almost indistinguishable and the dish takes on a unique flavour – much more than the taste of its many parts.

750 g (1 lb 11 oz) firm white fish fillets, such as snapper, mulloway, morwong (deep sea bream), mullet, ling or cod, cut into 7.5 cm (3 in) pieces

2 teaspoons turmeric

½–1 teaspoon salt, or to taste

2 tablespoons mustard oil

1 teaspoon panch phoron (page 12)

1 teaspoon ginger paste (page 12)

1 teaspoon garlic paste (page 12)

1 large onion, sliced

2 green chillies

8 small cauliflower florets

1 small red capsicum (pepper), sliced lengthwise

1 small green capsicum (pepper), sliced lengthwise

1 small yellow capsicum (pepper), sliced lengthwise

coriander (cilantro) leaves to garnish

Put the fish in a large bowl. Sprinkle with 1 teaspoon of the turmeric and the salt to taste, and toss together until the fish pieces are well coated.

Heat the mustard oil in a wok or large frying pan over a medium heat. When the oil is smoking, add the panch phoron, then immediately stir in the ginger and garlic pastes, onion and chillies. Immediately add the fish, cauliflower, red, green and yellow capsicum and remaining turmeric, and gently stir to coat.

Cover the wok, reduce the heat to as low as possible and cook for about 15 minutes, or until the fish and vegetables are just cooked – the timing will depend on the type and thickness of the fish. Resist the temptation to open the lid and stir the mixture, as this will break up the vegetables and fish.

Garnish with the coriander and serve hot.

Prawn Raita

Serves 4

If you think raita is just a cooling salad, then think again. I certainly had to when a cousin sent me an intriguing menu that she recently served on an important birthday in Kolkata (Calcutta). Forget the humble cucumber, try adding fresh prawns (shrimp) instead. This recipe works just as well with fresh oysters, mussels, crab meat or, my personal favourite, fabulously sweet rock lobster (crayfish). Make a summer meal with steamed basmati or other long-grain rice (see page 14) and a leafy green salad.

2 tablespoons mustard oil

2 green chillies, slit to just below the stalk area, top and seeds left intact

½ teaspoon panch phoron (page 12)

250 g (9 oz) tiger or medium raw prawns (shrimp), shelled and deveined

1 teaspoon black mustard seeds, crushed

½ teaspoon yellow mustard seeds, crushed

½–1 teaspoon salt, or to taste

250 g (9 oz/1 cup) plain yoghurt

½ teaspoon sugar

Heat the mustard oil in a large frying pan over a high heat. Wait until the oil starts to smoke (this gets rid of the pungent mustard flavour and releases a sweeter taste), then reduce the heat to medium. Stir in the green chillies and panch phoron and cook until the mixture crackles. Immediately add the prawns, black and yellow mustard seeds and salt and stir to mix through.

Cook over a medium heat for about 3 minutes, or until the prawns are translucent. Remove from the heat, place the mixture in a heatproof bowl and leave to cool in the refrigerator.

When the prawns are cool, mix together the yoghurt and sugar in a serving bowl until the sugar dissolves. Add the prawns, stir to mix through and serve cold.

Prawns with Vegetables and Panch Phoron

Serves 4

Some of the best recipes are never prepared in restaurants. This quick, healthy, easy and colourful dish from Bengal is a delicious example. Use raw prawns (shrimp) of any size. Often smaller prawns have a sweeter flavour, so don't be put off by the size and by thinking that bigger is better. Traditionally, the middle section of the prawn shell is removed for deveining, but the head and tail are left on for added flavour and crunch. The prawns are combined with a colourful medley of seasonal vegetables and served with steamed basmati or other long-grain rice (see page 14).

1 tablespoon mustard or other vegetable oil

2 green chillies, slit to just below the stalk area, top and seeds left intact

1 teaspoon panch phoron (page 12)

1 large onion, sliced

500 g (1 lb 2 oz) raw prawns (shrimp), washed thoroughly, shelled and deveined, heads and tails left intact, if desired

1 tablespoon ginger paste (page 12)

1 tablespoon garlic paste (page 12)

1 teaspoon turmeric

½–1 teaspoon salt, or to taste

2 cauliflower florets, thinly sliced

100 g (3½ oz) pumpkin (winter squash), such as butternut, jap or kent, peeled and diced

1 zucchini (courgette), diced

65 g (2¼ oz) frozen peas

50 g (1¾ oz) baby spinach leaves

6 green beans, trimmed

¼ red, green or yellow capsicum (pepper), thinly sliced lengthwise

100 g (3½ oz) finely shredded white cabbage

lime wedges to serve

Heat the oil in a wok or large frying pan over a medium heat. If you are using mustard oil, wait until it is smoking (this gets rid of the pungent mustard flavour and releases a sweeter taste). Stir in the green chillies and panch phoron and cook until the mixture crackles. Immediately add the onion, prawns, ginger and garlic pastes, turmeric and salt, increase the heat to high and stir-fry for 2 minutes.

Add the cauliflower, pumpkin, zucchini, peas, spinach, beans, capsicum and cabbage and stir to mix through. Reduce the heat to low, cover and cook until the prawns are translucent and firm to the bite – about 5 minutes for small prawns, 6 minutes for medium prawns and 7 minutes for large prawns. Serve hot, with lime wedges on the side for squeezing over.

Coconut and Coriander Fish Baked in Banana Leaves

Serves 4

A favourite from western India and a must at a Parsee wedding. This delicious recipe is one of the most popular dishes on the Spice Kitchen menu. It is especially loved by those who do not like their fish in a curry. You can serve it with steamed basmati or other long-grain rice (see page 14) or a leafy green salad.

4 × 200 g (7 oz) thick firm fish fillets, such as snapper, mullet, mulloway, kingfish, barramundi, bream, perch, salmon, ling, cod or other meaty fish

4 pieces of banana leaf (each about twice the size of the fish fillet), washed (see Note)

100 ml (3½ fl oz) white vinegar

2 tablespoons vegetable or canola oil

lime cheeks to serve

Coconut and Coriander Paste

½ teaspoon ginger paste (page 12)

½ teaspoon garlic paste (page 12)

45 g (1½ oz/½ cup) desiccated (grated dried) coconut

2 green chillies

1 teaspoon ground cumin

juice of 1 lemon

½ cup coriander (cilantro) leaves

½–1 teaspoon salt, or to taste

Preheat the oven to 180°C (350°F).

To make the coconut and coriander paste, blend the ginger and garlic pastes, coconut, chillies, cumin, lemon juice, coriander and salt in a food processor until it forms a smooth paste.

Coat the fish fillets thoroughly with the paste. Put each fillet in the middle of a piece of banana leaf and wrap it up: fold in the end closest to you first, then the sides, then fold over the top.

Mix together the vinegar and oil in a shallow baking dish, then carefully put the fish parcels, folded side down, in the dish.

Cook in the oven for about 15 minutes. Carefully unwrap the parcel to check that the fish is ready – it should be just cooked and moist, and flake easily when pressed. Serve hot, with the lime cheeks on the side for squeezing over.

Note: If banana leaves are not available, you could try lotus leaves for a different flavour, or simply use baking paper.

Baked Mustard Fish

Serves 4

The good folk of Bengal have a reputation for arguing about everything, and food is no exception. A unanimous decision on the best fish curry could never be made, although baked mustard fish would be a strong contender. In fact, this is a Bengal recipe with a cult following, although it does have fairly strong flavours and plenty of heat, and of course, you have to like mustard. If you tick all those boxes, there is no better fish recipe. It is usually baked, but can also be steamed. Serve it with steamed basmati rice (see page 14).

1 kg (2 lb 3 oz) firm white fish fillets, such as snapper, morwong (deep sea bream), perch, kingfish, ling or cod, or small whole fish, such as garfish, tommy ruff, sardines or mackerel

Mustard Paste

½ teaspoon turmeric

1 tablespoon yellow mustard seeds, coarsely crushed

1 tablespoon black mustard seeds, coarsely crushed

1 teaspoon hot English mustard

2 tablespoons mustard oil

1 tablespoon plain yoghurt

4 green chillies

½–1 teaspoon salt, or to taste

If baking the fish in the oven, preheat the oven to 170°C (340°).

To make the mustard paste, mix together the turmeric, yellow and black mustard seeds, hot English mustard, mustard oil, yoghurt, chillies and salt in a large bowl.

Add the fish to the bowl and stir to coat thoroughly with the mustard paste.

Put the fish with the paste in a shallow baking dish with a lid. Cover tightly and cook in the oven for about 20 minutes for fillets, and 30 minutes for small whole fish. The fish should be just cooked – the flesh should flake easily and be very soft and moist. Serve hot.

Alternatively, put the fish with the paste in a shallow heatproof dish or bowl. Carefully put the dish or bowl in a metal or bamboo steamer. Place in a saucepan or wok of water simmering over a low heat, making sure that the water level is below the fish. Cover and steam over a low heat for 25 minutes for fillets, and 30 minutes for small whole fish. Check the simmering water during cooking and add more as it evaporates, but make sure the water level is always below the fish.

Carefully remove the fish from the steamer and serve hot.

Prawn Masala

Serves 4

This simple North Indian prawn (shrimp) dish is deliciously different from the coconut curries of South and West India, and is very popular in restaurants because it is quite easy to make and it does not need a lot of spices. The tomato–capsicum (–pepper) combination is delectable and appeals to a wide range of taste buds. Serve with steamed basmati or other long-grain rice (see page 14) and Naan (page 200).

1 kg (2 lb 3 oz) medium or large
  raw prawns (shrimp), shelled
  and deveined

1 teaspoon turmeric

½–1 teaspoon salt, or to taste

2 tablespoons vegetable or
  canola oil

1 onion, sliced

1 tablespoon ginger paste
  (page 12)

1 tablespoon garlic paste
  (page 12)

2 green chillies

1 tablespoon ground coriander

1 teaspoon chilli powder

6 tomatoes, diced, or
  1.5 x 400 g (14 oz) cans
  diced tomatoes, drained

2 yellow, red or green
  capsicums (peppers), diced

coriander (cilantro) leaves to
  garnish

Put the prawns in a large bowl. Sprinkle over the turmeric and salt and toss to thoroughly coat the prawns. Set aside.

Heat the oil in a large frying pan. Sauté the onion over a medium heat, stirring occasionally, for 6–8 minutes, or until golden brown. Stir in the ginger and garlic pastes and the green chillies, and cook for 2 minutes.

Add the ground coriander and chilli powder and cook, stirring, for about 1 minute, or until the spices release their aroma. Add the tomato and capsicum and cook over a medium heat, stirring occasionally, for about 4 minutes, or until the tomato has softened.

Add the reserved prawns and cook, stirring occasionally, until the prawns are translucent and firm to the bite – about 5 minutes for medium prawns and 7 minutes for large prawns.

Garnish with the coriander leaves and serve hot.

Scampi Kerala Curry

Serves 4

For me, this recipe conjures up images of rice barges floating along the backwaters of Kerala, which are teeming with fresh scampi. Boatmen catch the scampi with nets and make this delicious curry for everyone on board. The aromas of this dish always transport me to such a paradise. Serve this dish with steamed basmati or other long-grain rice (see page 14), or for something really special, the red short-grain rice from Kerala.

100 ml (3½ fl oz) coconut oil (see Notes) or other vegetable oil

½ teaspoon fenugreek seeds

6 garlic cloves, crushed

8 spring onions (scallions), sliced

2 x 3 cm (1¼ in) pieces fresh ginger, julienned

4 green chillies, slit to just below the stalk area, top and seeds left intact

20 curry leaves

20 g (¾ oz) kokum, soaked and chopped (see Notes), or 2 tablespoons tamarind pulp (page 14)

½–1 teaspoon salt, or to taste

800 g (1 lb 12 oz) fresh scampi

200 ml (7 fl oz) fresh coconut milk (page 14) or canned coconut milk

Paste

1 tablespoon chilli powder

½ tablespoon ground coriander

½ teaspoon turmeric

½ teaspoon ginger paste (page 12)

½ teaspoon garlic paste (page 12)

To make the paste, mix the chilli powder, coriander, turmeric and ginger and garlic pastes together with 1–2 tablespoons water in a small bowl until it forms a paste. Set aside.

Heat the oil in a large saucepan over a medium heat. Cook the fenugreek seeds for about 5 seconds, until they become light brown. Immediately stir in the crushed garlic and cook for about 30 seconds, or until golden brown.

Add the paste and sauté, stirring continuously, for a further 2–3 minutes. Add the spring onion, ginger, green chillies, curry leaves, kokum or tamarind, salt and 250 ml (8½ fl oz/1 cup) water. Stir to mix together, then bring to a boil.

Add the scampi, cover and cook over a medium heat for about 8 minutes, or until the sauce thickens.

Stir in the coconut milk, reduce the heat to low and cook uncovered for a further 2 minutes. Serve hot.

Notes: If using coconut oil, make sure it is fresh. Like olive oil, coconut oil can become rancid if it is not stored properly or if it is old. Fresh coconut oil has a lovely sweet flavour but it can absolutely spoil a dish if it is stale.

Kokum is the dried rind of the fruit of the kokum tree. It is found in Indian or Asian grocery stores. Make sure that it is soft and pliable, and only buy a small quantity as it tends to dry up if kept for too long.

Crab Malabar

Serves 4

Contrary to common perception, there are hundreds of seafood recipes in India. Fried, grilled (broiled), poached in oil, poached in water, steamed, curried, wrapped in banana leaves – from Kashmir, Bengal, Maharashtra, Goa and Kerala, you are sure to find a recipe to get you salivating. This recipe comes from the Malabar Coast, which abounds with seafood. You can use blue swimmer crabs, mud crabs or spanner crabs. Serve with steamed basmati or other long-grain rice (see page 14).

4 fresh crabs (big enough to serve 1 per person)

2 tablespoons vegetable or canola oil

1 small onion, sliced

3 green chillies, slit to just below the stalk area, top and seeds left intact

45 g (1½ oz/½ cup) desiccated (grated dried) coconut or 60 g (2 oz) freshly grated coconut

1 large onion, puréed in a food processor until smooth, or finely grated

1 tablespoon ginger paste (page 12)

1 tablespoon garlic paste (page 12)

2 tablespoons ground coriander

1 teaspoon chilli powder

1 teaspoon turmeric

3 tomatoes, chopped

½–1 teaspoon salt, or to taste

If you are using live crabs (which give the best results), desensitise them first by placing them in the freezer for 20 minutes.

Remove from the freezer and separate the hard shell from the body. Remove the grey, crunchy, finger-like bits. Separate the claws from the body – these are easy to break off blue swimmer crabs, but you may need to use a cleaver for crabs such as mud or spanner crabs. Divide the crab body into four smaller pieces – either use a cleaver to divide them, or gently break them into quarters with your hands. Set aside.

Heat the oil in a large saucepan over a medium heat. Sauté the sliced onion and green chillies, stirring occasionally, for about 5 minutes, or until the onion is golden brown. Add the coconut and stir for a further 1 minute. Add the onion purée and ginger and garlic pastes and sauté for 5 minutes, stirring occasionally.

Add the coriander, chilli powder, turmeric, tomato and salt, and cook over a medium heat, stirring occasionally, for about 7 minutes, or until the tomato has softened.

Add all the crab pieces, along with 125–250 ml (4–8½ fl oz/½–1 cup) water, then stir to mix through. Reduce the heat to low, cover the saucepan with the lid and simmer for 20 minutes, or until the crab meat is firm and translucent. Serve hot.

Spicy Fish Chaat

Serves 4

This is a wonderful dish for a light lunch or as a starter before dinner. Chaat is the word used for a mixture that has piquant, tantalising flavours with contrasting crisp, crumbly and soft textures, and is mainly vegetarian. In North India chaat is available from specialist cafés and street vendors, many of whom have a cult following. The ingredients used in this recipe combine to achieve an intriguing balance of contrasting and complementary flavours. It can be served hot or at room temperature.

800 g (1 lb 12 oz) firm white fish fillets, such as snapper, mullet, barramundi, mulloway, ling, cod or other meaty fish, cut into 2.5 cm (1 in) pieces

vegetable or canola oil for deep-frying

2 medium or 1 large cucumber, diced

1 red (Spanish) onion, chopped

1 teaspoon chaat masala (page 11)

juice of 2 lemons or limes

Tamarind and Ginger Chutney (page 186)

Mint Chutney (page 187)

Marinade

2 tablespoons white vinegar

1 tablespoon ginger paste (page 12)

1 tablespoon garlic paste (page 12)

1 teaspoon chilli powder

½ teaspoon ground white pepper

½–1 teaspoon salt, or to taste

30 g (1 oz/¼ cup) besan (chickpea flour)

Put the fish in a large bowl. Sprinkle in the marinade ingredients one by one: the vinegar, ginger paste, garlic paste, chilli powder, white pepper, salt and besan. Toss to thoroughly coat the fish in the marinade, then cover and put in the refrigerator to marinate for up to 20 minutes.

Heat the oil in a wok or deep-fryer to 180°C (350°F) (see page 15). Deep-fry the fish a few pieces at a time for about 2 minutes, or until crispy on the outside and the flesh flakes easily when pressed. Remove from the oil and drain on kitchen towels.

Put the fried fish in a large serving bowl. Add the cucumber and onion and carefully toss through. Sprinkle with the chaat masala and pour over the lemon or lime juice.

Drizzle with the tamarind and ginger chutney and mint chutney and serve immediately or at room temperature.

Prawn Malai Curry

Serves 4

This very famous prawn curry from Bengal is the most requested dish for special occasions in my family. Use the largest freshest prawns (shrimp) you can find. The heads contain fabulous flavour and are considered a delicacy in India. Even if you do not want to eat them, try leaving the shells on until the curry is cooked, and then remove them – they will deliver loads of additional flavour. The Hindi word for cream is malai, referring to the coconut creaminess of the sauce. Serve with steamed rice (see page 14).

1 kg (2 lb 3 oz) raw large prawns (shrimp), washed thoroughly, shelled and deveined if desired

2 teaspoons turmeric

½–1 teaspoon salt, or to taste

vegetable or canola oil for deep-frying

Sauce

4 green cardamom pods

2.5 cm (1 in) cinnamon stick

4 cloves

1 large onion, chopped

2 teaspoons ginger paste (page 12)

2 teaspoons garlic paste (page 12)

1 teaspoon turmeric

1 teaspoon chilli powder

½ teaspoon sugar

½–1 teaspoon salt, or to taste

2 large potatoes, peeled and cut into cubes

250 ml (8½ fl oz/1 cup) fresh coconut milk (page 14) or canned coconut milk (see Note)

Put the prawns in a large bowl. Sprinkle with the turmeric and salt and toss to thoroughly coat the prawns.

Heat the oil in a wok or deep-fryer to 180°C (350°F) (see page 15). Deep-fry the prawns a few at a time to seal, about 2 minutes. Transfer to a plate and set aside.

Pour off most of the oil, leaving about 2 tablespoons in the wok. Heat this remaining oil over a medium heat. Add the cardamom pods, cinnamon, cloves and onion and sauté, stirring occasionally, for about 4 minutes or until the onion is golden brown. Add the ginger and garlic pastes, turmeric, chilli powder, sugar and salt and cook, stirring, for 2 minutes.

Add 125 ml (4 fl oz/½ cup) water, then stir in the potato. Reduce the heat to low, cover and simmer for 10 minutes.

Stir in the coconut milk and then return the deep-fried prawns to the wok. Reduce the heat to very low, cover and simmer, stirring occasionally, for a further 10 minutes. The potato should be soft and the prawns translucent and firm to the bite. Serve hot.

Note: Canned coconut milk will suffice, but if you can make your own with freshly grated coconut steeped in hot water and sieved, you'll taste the difference. For this recipe, you will need 100 g (3½ oz/2 cups) of freshly grated coconut and 375 ml (12½ fl oz/1½ cups) warm water (see page 14).

Prawns with Zucchini

Serves 4

This dish of prawns (shrimp) with zucchini (courgette) has a hint of spice and the clean pure flavours of Bengal. Serve simply with steamed basmati rice (see page 14). If you feel like spoiling yourself, this is a lovely recipe to downsize and make for just one person.

500 g (1 lb 2 oz) small or medium raw prawns (shrimp), shelled and deveined

2 teaspoons turmeric, plus an extra pinch

½–1 teaspoon salt, plus an extra pinch

1 tablespoon mustard oil

1 tablespoon ginger paste (page 12)

2 green chillies

8 small zucchini (courgettes) or green marrow (soft squash), peeled and diced (see Note)

Put the prawns in a large bowl. Sprinkle with 2 teaspoons of the turmeric and ½–1 teaspoon of the salt and toss to thoroughly coat the prawns.

Heat the mustard oil in a wok or large frying pan over a medium heat. When it is smoking, cook the ginger paste and chillies for about 30 seconds, stirring continuously. Add the prawns and cook, stirring occasionally, until translucent – about 5 minutes for small prawns and 8 minutes for medium prawns.

Stir in the zucchini or green marrow with the extra turmeric and salt. Reduce the heat to low, cover and cook for about 10 minutes, or until the zucchini is soft. Serve hot.

Note: This recipe requires a total of 300 g (10½ oz/2 cups) of diced zucchini or green marrow.

POULTRY

Chicken is still the most popular meat eaten in India. Every family has a favourite secret chicken recipe and restaurants can become famous for a particular chicken dish they serve. Customers may queue up for hours to taste Tandoori Chicken (page 112) – grilled in a traditional charcoal tandoor, or wait patiently for their favourite Butter Chicken (page 128) from another restaurant. Hole-in-the-wall eateries may attract people from miles around for their Chicken Biryani (page 114).

At home chicken is relatively easy to prepare and takes much less time to cook than red meat. It lends itself to many different Indian cooking styles – cooked whole, or jointed or boneless, quickly grilled (broiled) or wok fried, or even minced (ground) and made into delectable koftas.

Chicken teams up well with a diverse range of spices to produce regional specialties – from a rich and delicate Saffron Chicken Korma (page 116) to a hot and spicy Karahi Chicken (page 124). In the south coconut and almonds impart a creaminess to chicken dishes, while in the north chicken features largely in Indian street food.

In addition to tandoori chicken and biryani – you may use grilled chicken with a tandoori marinade in wraps or enjoy South Indian Fried Chicken (page 118) with its delicate flavour of curry leaves.

You can substitute other poultry, such as quail, duck, pheasant or spatchcock in these recipes, but whichever poultry you choose make sure it is free range for the best taste and texture.

Tandoori Chicken

Serves 4

India's original fast food, tandoori chicken, can be cooked on a barbecue or in an oven. However, it is difficult to produce the fabulous, smoky, charcoal-scented flavour of this dish without a charcoal oven. The tandoor, a clay oven fired with charcoal, was introduced into North-West India during Mughal rule (1526–1858). Today, tandoori-style food is an important facet of Indian cooking and modern tandoors are made of stainless steel and insulated with fibreglass and fired by gas. For a complete meal, serve this dish with a leafy green or garden salad and Naan (page 200).

1 x 800 g–1 kg
  (1 lb 12 oz–2 lb 3 oz) chicken

juice of 1 lemon

pinch of salt

1½ teaspoons chilli powder

ghee (page 13) or salted butter
  for basting

lemon wedges to garnish

sliced red (Spanish) onion
  to garnish

Marinade

1 teaspoon ginger paste
  (page 12)

1 teaspoon garlic paste
  (page 12)

60 g (2 oz/¼ cup) plain yoghurt

1 teaspoon garam masala
  (page 11)

pinch of tandoori colour
  (see Note)

pinch of whole mace

Remove the skin from the chicken and make small incisions in the body and legs with a sharp knife. Place on a shallow dish or plate and rub with the lemon juice, salt and chilli powder. Put in the refrigerator for 20 minutes.

To make the marinade, mix together the ginger and garlic pastes, yoghurt, garam masala, tandoori colour and mace in a small bowl. Coat the chicken with the marinade and marinate in the refrigerator for a further 4 hours.

Preheat the oven to 250°C (480°F). Remove the chicken from the marinade and put in a roasting tin. Cook in the oven for about 30–40 minutes, turning and basting with the ghee or butter every 10 minutes, until the chicken is cooked.

Alternatively, preheat a gas barbecue with a lid to high, or a charcoal barbecue with a lid until the charcoal or barbecue fuel briquettes become red embers. Insert a metal rod through the chicken and place it on a flat tray. Put the tray on the barbecue, close the lid and cook for about 30–40 minutes, turning and basting with the ghee or butter every 10 minutes, until the chicken is cooked.

To check if the chicken is cooked through, insert a knife into the joint dividing the thigh and the drumstick. If the juices that run out are clear, the chicken is cooked – any signs of blood or a pinkish liquid means the chicken needs further cooking.

Cut the chicken into 8 pieces with a very sharp knife or cleaver, garnish with the lemon wedges and onion slices and serve.

Note: Tandoori colour is an Indian food colouring that has no taste. You can buy it in Indian grocery stores.

Chicken Biryani

Serves 4

This is a special rice and chicken dish, and a complete meal in itself – a one-dish entertainer for a casual evening, or for lunch on the veranda. Any alfresco setting will do! My memory takes me back to warm, moonlit nights and picnics in lush tropical gardens shadowed by mysterious ruins of civilisations long gone. This biryani recipe is different from other versions that use lamb and vegetables. Its origins are in Persia, and when you prepare it, the flavour and fragrance will fill the whole room. The only accompaniment it needs is some Dahi Chutney (page 192).

75 g (2¾ oz/½ cup) Fried Onions (page 209)

large handful coriander (cilantro) leaves, chopped

large handful mint leaves, chopped

1 teaspoon saffron infusion (page 13)

1 teaspoon turmeric

hard-boiled eggs to garnish

sultanas (golden raisins) to garnish

unsalted roasted cashew nuts, slivered almonds, shelled pistachio nuts or pine nuts to garnish

Rice

200 g (7 oz/1 cup) basmati rice or other long-grain rice, washed and drained

4 bay leaves

4 black peppercorns

4 cloves

2 green cardamom pods

2.5 cm (1 in) cinnamon stick

Chicken

1 x 1 kg (2 lb 3 oz) chicken

2 tablespoons vegetable or canola oil

2 bay leaves

3 black peppercorns

3 cloves

4 green cardamom pods

2.5 cm (1 in) cinnamon stick

1 tablespoon whole mace

2 green chillies

1 large onion, chopped

1 tablespoon ginger paste (page 12)

1 tablespoon garlic paste (page 12)

125 g (4 oz/½ cup) plain yoghurt

1 large tomato, cut into wedges

½–1 teaspoon salt, or to taste

To prepare the rice, put it in a large heavy-based saucepan with the bay leaves, peppercorns, cloves, cardamom pods and cinnamon and 1 litre (34 fl oz/4 cups) water. Bring to a boil, then cook uncovered over a high heat for 15 minutes, or until parboiled. Drain and set aside.

Meanwhile, to prepare the chicken, joint or cut it into eight serving pieces with a very sharp knife or a cleaver. To do this, remove the legs from the breast section and divide each leg into two pieces – the thigh and the drumstick. Halve the breast section lengthwise along the breastbone, then cut crosswise in half again.

Continue preparing the chicken. Heat the oil in a large heavy-based saucepan over a medium heat. Add the bay leaves, peppercorns, cloves, cardamom pods, cinnamon, mace and green chillies, and cook, stirring continuously, for about 1 minute, or until the spices release their aroma. Stir in the onion and sauté for about 2 minutes, or until golden brown. Stir in the ginger and garlic pastes and cook for a further 2 minutes. Add the chicken pieces, yoghurt, tomato and salt and stir to mix through. Cover and cook over a medium heat for 30 minutes, or until cooked through.

Preheat the oven to 180°C (350°F).

In a casserole dish, arrange layers of the rice, chicken, fried onions, coriander and mint, finishing with a top layer of the rice. Mix together the saffron infusion and turmeric in a small bowl, then carefully pour it into one corner of the dish. Cover and cook in the oven for 20 minutes.

Garnish with the hard-boiled eggs, sultanas and nuts and serve.

Saffron Chicken Korma

Serves 4

The ancient Mughals laid down the foundations of classical Indian cuisine. They set up huge kitchens, staffed with hundreds of cooks, who vied with each other to produce innovative dishes using new techniques and ingredients. Korma comes from the word 'quarama', which means 'braising in oil'. Kormas are mild, delicate and rich curries, best enjoyed in small quantities. Serve the korma with Pulao Rice (page 167) and Parathas (page 206) or Chapattis (page 202).

30 g (1 oz) ghee (page 13) or 2 tablespoons vegetable or canola oil

½ teaspoon whole mace

4 green cardamom pods

2.5 cm (1 in) cinnamon stick

3 cloves

1 whole dried red chilli

1 small onion, chopped

1 tablespoon ginger paste (page 12)

3 teaspoons garlic paste (page 12)

½ teaspoon turmeric

2 teaspoons coriander seeds, ground

60 g (2 oz/¼ cup) plain yoghurt

½–1 teaspoon salt, or to taste

1 kg (2 lb 3 oz) boneless, skinless chicken thighs, each cut into 6 pieces

½ teaspoon saffron infusion (page 13)

125 ml (4 fl oz/½ cup) pouring (single/light) cream

55 g (2 oz/½ cup) ground almonds

unsalted roasted cashew nuts to garnish

sultanas (golden raisins) to garnish

Heat the ghee or oil in a large heavy-based saucepan over a medium heat. Sauté the mace, cardamom pods, cinnamon, cloves, chilli and onion, stirring occasionally, for about 15 minutes or until the onion is golden brown. Stir in the ginger and garlic pastes and cook, stirring frequently, for about 2 minutes. Add the turmeric and coriander and cook, stirring, for 1 minute.

Stir in the yoghurt and salt and cook for 1 minute. Add the chicken and stir to mix through, then reduce the heat to low, cover and cook for 30 minutes.

Stir the saffron infusion, cream and ground almonds through the korma. Cover again, reduce the heat to very low and cook for about 10 minutes, or until the korma has thickened.

Garnish with the nuts and sultanas. Serve hot.

Saag Chicken

Serves 4

This home-style recipe is healthier than many of the restaurant versions of this dish, and it does not use bicarbonate of soda (baking soda) to retain the green colour of the spinach – as is the usual practice in commerical Indian cooking. As a result, this dish preserves all the vegetable's vitamins and minerals. The combination of chicken with spinach works really well, with the spinach providing a thick base and a fresh, slightly astringent taste to the curry. Serve it with Pulao Rice (page 167) and Parathas (page 206) or Chapattis (page 202).

60 ml (2 fl oz/¼ cup) vegetable or canola oil

1 large onion, chopped

1 tablespoon ginger paste (page 12)

1 tablespoon garlic paste (page 12)

2 tablespoons plain yoghurt

1 teaspoon ground coriander

1 teaspoon chilli powder

1 teaspoon dried fenugreek leaves

½–1 teaspoon salt, or to taste

1 kg (2 lb 3 oz) boneless, skinless chicken thighs, each cut into 6 pieces

600 g (1 lb 5 oz) English spinach, washed thoroughly and roughly chopped

Heat the oil in a large heavy-based saucepan over a medium heat. Sauté the onion, stirring occasionally, for about 5–7 minutes, or until brown. Stir in the ginger and garlic pastes and cook for 2 minutes.

Stir in the yoghurt, coriander, chilli powder, fenugreek leaves and salt. Add up to 125 ml (4 fl oz/½ cup) water, 1 tablespoon at a time, until the mixture forms a thick sauce.

Add the chicken, stir to mix through the sauce, then cover, reduce the heat to low and simmer for about 30 minutes, or until the chicken is three-quarters cooked.

Stir in the spinach, then cover and simmer for a further 6 minutes, or until the spinach is cooked.

Alternatively, if you prefer the spinach to form a really smooth purée, blanch the spinach in a large saucepan of boiling water for 2 minutes. Drain, allow to cool a little, then purée in a food processor. Add the spinach purée to the three-quarters-cooked chicken and stir through, then cover and simmer for 2–3 minutes to heat through. Serve hot.

South Indian Fried Chicken

Serves 4

On the roads between the big towns and cities of South India – Chennai, Bangalore, Kochi, Trivandrum, Ooty – you can find many cafés selling this spicy chicken dish wrapped in banana leaves or paper. Open the parcel and you will be engulfed in a magical fragrance that will leave your average fried chicken for dead! Serve this dish with a leafy green salad.

1 kg (2 lb 3 oz) boneless, skinless chicken thighs, each cut into 4 pieces

50 g (2 oz) besan (chickpea flour)

25 g (1 oz) plain (all-purpose) flour

vegetable or canola oil for deep-frying

lime wedges to serve

Marinade

25 curry leaves, chopped

2 tablespoons ginger paste (page 12)

4 tablespoons garlic paste (page 12)

5 green chillies, chopped

1 teaspoon chilli powder

juice of 2 lemons

½–1 teaspoon salt, or to taste

Put the chicken in a large bowl. Sprinkle in the marinade ingredients one by one: the curry leaves, ginger paste, garlic paste, green chilli, chilli powder, lemon juice and salt. Stir to thoroughly coat the chicken pieces, then cover and put in the refrigerator to marinate for 1 hour.

Add the besan and plain flour to the chicken and mix well.

Heat the oil in a wok or deep-fryer to 180°C (350°F) (see page 15). Deep-fry the chicken a few pieces at a time for 8–10 minutes, or until crisp on the outside and cooked through. Drain on kitchen towels and serve immediately with lime wedges.

Chicken Pasanda Roll

Serves 4

Indian food isn't all about curries, good as they are. I find that sometimes, I feel like something with a touch of spice but not in a sauce. This recipe fits the bill perfectly. It is a special chicken and panir cheese roll, which serves as a starter or as part of an Indian banquet. Slice thickly and serve with Sesame Chutney (page 192).

8 boneless chicken thighs, skin left on

mint leaves to garnish

Marinade

1 tablespoon white vinegar

125 g (4½ oz/½ cup) plain yoghurt

1 teaspoon ground white pepper

1 teaspoon ginger paste (page 12)

1 teaspoon garlic paste (page 12)

60 ml (2 fl oz/¼ cup) vegetable or canola oil

½–1 teaspoon salt, or to taste

Stuffing

1 green chilli, chopped

½ small red (Spanish) onion, chopped

150 g (5½ oz) panir cheese (page 13), crumbled

½ teaspoon freshly ground whole mace

½ teaspoon ground cardamom

2 tablespoons cornflour (cornstarch)

1 egg

½–1 teaspoon salt, or to taste

Score the skin of the chicken pieces with a very sharp knife, then flatten with a meat mallet or the flat of a large knife or cleaver. Put the chicken in a shallow dish.

To make the marinade, mix together the vinegar, yoghurt, white pepper, ginger and garlic pastes, oil and salt in a small bowl. Pour the marinade over the chicken and coat well on both sides, then marinate in the refrigerator for 2 hours.

Preheat the oven to 200°C (400°F).

To make the stuffing, mix together the chilli, onion, panir cheese, mace, cardamom, cornflour, egg and salt in a medium bowl.

Wet your hands and divide the mixture into eight portions. Shape each portion into a cylinder, about 2 cm (¾ in) in diameter and the length of a flattened piece of the chicken.

Lay a marinated piece of chicken skin side down on the work surface. Put a cylinder of stuffing at one end and roll up the chicken to enclose the stuffing. Tie firmly with kitchen string. Repeat for the remaining cylinders of stuffing and marinated chicken pieces.

Put the stuffed chicken rolls in a roasting tin. Spread any left-over marinade over the top, then cook in the oven for about 20 minutes, or until the chicken is cooked through. To test that it is done, make a small incision in the chicken with a sharp knife – it should be white and firm, with no pinkness.

Rest for 10 minutes before removing the string from each roll. Slice thickly and serve with mint leaves sprinkled over the top.

Chicken Methi

Serves 4

When planted, fenugreek seeds sprout fenugreek leaves, which are similar to watercress and have a lovely fresh, sharp flavour with a hint of bitterness. Methi refers to fenugreek leaves, fresh or dried, and they are used in salads, dals and with potatoes to make methi alu – a favourite recipe of North India. It is the use of dried fenugreek leaves together with fresh English spinach leaves that gives this curry its distinctive flavour – a slightly bitter, astringent taste mellowed by tomato. This dish is good served with Parathas (page 206), Chapattis (page 202) or Naan (page 200).

600 g (1 lb 5 oz) English spinach leaves, stalks discarded, washed thoroughly and roughly chopped

2 tablespoons vegetable or canola oil

1 small onion, chopped

1 tablespoon ginger paste (page 12)

1 tablespoon garlic paste (page 12)

1 tablespoon ground coriander

1 teaspoon turmeric

1 teaspoon chilli powder

1 tomato, chopped

1 kg (2 lb 3 oz) boneless, skinless chicken thighs, each cut into 3 cm (1¼ in) pieces

1½ tablespoons dried fenugreek leaves

½–1 teaspoon salt, or to taste

Cook the spinach in 125 ml (4 fl oz/½ cup) water in a large uncovered saucepan over a high heat for 5 minutes. Drain and allow to cool a little, then purée in a food processor and set aside.

Heat the oil in a large heavy-based saucepan over a medium heat. Sauté the onion, stirring occasionally, for about 2 minutes, or until golden brown. Add the ginger and garlic pastes and sauté, stirring, for 2 minutes.

Stir in the coriander, turmeric, chilli powder and tomato and cook for 10 seconds. Add the chicken and stir, then cover the saucepan, reduce the heat to low and cook for about 30 minutes, or until the chicken is almost done.

Stir in the puréed spinach, fenugreek leaves and salt and cook for a further 2 minutes. Serve hot.

Chicken Masala

Serves 4

The Spice Kitchen started with a basic chicken masala recipe on the menu twenty-four years ago. Despite many other changes in the restaurant, the chicken masala remains unaltered as it is a firm favourite! A traditional North Indian recipe, chicken masala works well as an everyday meal or served with all the trimmings and a vegetable biryani for a special occasion. This recipe is traditionally made with ground spices as this is faster and easier. Serve with steamed basmati or other long-grain rice (see page 14).

2 tablespoons vegetable or canola oil

1 large onion, chopped

2 tablespoons ground coriander

1 tablespoon ground cumin

1 teaspoon chilli powder

1 teaspoon turmeric

1 tablespoon ginger paste (page 12)

1 tablespoon garlic paste (page 12)

2 tablespoons plain yoghurt

1 kg (2 lb 3 oz) boneless, skinless chicken thighs, each cut into 3 pieces

½–1 teaspoon salt, or to taste

chopped coriander (cilantro) leaves to garnish

Heat the oil in a large heavy-based saucepan over a medium heat. Sauté the onion, stirring occasionally, for about 5 minutes, or until golden brown.

Meanwhile, mix together the ground coriander, cumin, chilli powder and turmeric with 1–2 teaspoons water in a small bowl to make a paste.

Add the ginger and garlic pastes to the onion and cook, stirring, for 2 minutes, then add the spice paste and stir for 10 seconds.

Stir in the yoghurt, chicken and salt. The resulting sauce should have the consistency of a thick soup. If necessary, add up to 125 ml (4 fl oz/½ cup) water, 2 teaspoons at a time, to obtain this consistency. (Some yoghurts have a runnier consistency than others.) Cover and simmer over a low heat for about 30 minutes, or until the chicken is cooked and tender.

Garnish with the chopped coriander and serve.

Karahi Chicken

Serves 4

Cooking with a karahi, or Indian wok, is a special cooking method that originated hundreds of years ago in North-West India. The coarsely crushed spices, the intensity of heat and the super-speedy cooking that are a feature of this style of cuisine give karahi cooking its distinctive flavour. Karahi chicken is the original karahi recipe. Constant stirring is the key to success. Serve it with Naan (page 200), Parathas (page 206) or Chapattis (page 202).

2 tablespoons vegetable or canola oil

1 onion, chopped

½ teaspoon ginger paste (page 12)

½ teaspoon garlic paste (page 12)

2 green chillies, chopped

4 tablespoons balti masala (page 12)

½ teaspoon turmeric

500 g (1 lb 2 oz) skinless, boneless chicken thighs, each cut into 2 cm (¾ in) pieces

1 small green capsicum (pepper), diced

1 small red capsicum (pepper), diced

2 ripe tomatoes, chopped

2 tablespoons chopped coriander (cilantro) leaves

½–1 teaspoon salt, or to taste

Heat the oil in a wok, karahi or large frying pan over a high heat. Stir-fry the onion for about 2 minutes, or until translucent.

Add the ginger and garlic pastes and stir-fry for 30 seconds. Add the chilli, balti masala and turmeric and stir-fry for 30 seconds. Add the chicken and stir-fry to coat with the spice mixture, then stir in the green and red capsicum and cook for 10 seconds.

Add the tomato, chopped coriander and salt and continue to cook over a high heat, stirring continuously, for about 20–25 minutes, or until the chicken is cooked. (You will need to keep stirring constantly throughout the cooking time.) Serve hot.

Chicken Kofta Korma

Serves 4

These chicken koftas are to die for – delicate, melt in the mouth and unforgettable. Many kofta recipes use red meat and are fried, but the best koftas are poached in sauce and have a lovely tender juiciness. This recipe uses a korma sauce, rich with yoghurt, cream and ground almonds – save it for a special occasion and serve it with Pulao Rice (page 167) and Naan (page 200), Parathas (page 206) or Chapattis (page 202).

Koftas

500 g (1 lb 2 oz) minced (ground) chicken

1 onion, chopped

1 tablespoon ginger paste (page 12)

1 tablespoon garlic paste (page 12)

80 g (2¾ oz/1 cup) fresh breadcrumbs

2 eggs

½–1 teaspoon salt, or to taste

1 teaspoon chopped coriander (cilantro) leaves

1 teaspoon chopped mint leaves

½ teaspoon ground cardamom

½ teaspoon freshly ground whole mace

Sauce

60 g (2 oz) ghee (page 13) or salted butter (see Note)

2 large onions, sliced

1 dried whole red chilli

1 tablespoon ginger paste (page 12)

1 teaspoon garlic paste (page 12)

1 teaspoon turmeric

1 teaspoon ground coriander

60 g (2 oz /¼ cup) plain yoghurt

125 ml (4 fl oz/½ cup) pouring (single/light) cream

½–1 teaspoon salt, or to taste

1 tablespoon ground almonds

To make the koftas, mix together the chicken, onion, ginger and garlic pastes, breadcrumbs, eggs, salt, coriander and mint leaves, cardamom and mace in a large bowl. Dip your hands in warm water and, using the palms of your hands, roll the kofta mixture into balls about 3 cm (1¼ in) in diameter. Set aside.

To make the sauce, heat the ghee or butter in a large heavy-based saucepan over a medium heat. Sauté the onion and chilli, stirring occasionally, for about 5 minutes, or until the onion is golden brown.

Stir in the ginger and garlic pastes and cook, stirring frequently, for about 2 minutes. Add the turmeric, ground coriander and yoghurt and cook, stirring occasionally, for 3 minutes.

Stir in the cream, salt and 250 ml (8½ fl oz/1 cup) water and bring to a boil, then immediately reduce the heat to low and simmer uncovered for 10 minutes. Add the ground almonds and cook for a further 5 minutes.

Carefully drop the koftas into the sauce, then cover and cook over a low heat for 30 minutes. Serve hot.

Note: Ghee really is preferable for this recipe as it has the best flavour and consistency. You can replace it with salted butter, but the final flavour will not be as nuanced or as rich.

Butter Chicken

Serves 4

In contrast to other regional Indian dishes, butter chicken is a relative newcomer, being only about fifty years old. Today, it is one of the most popular dishes in the Indian repertoire. Traditionally cooked in a tandoor clay oven, its smoky flavour, combined with a sweetish tomato sauce and contrasted with bitter fenugreek leaves, appeals to many palates. Serve with hot Naan (page 200).

1 kg (2 lb 3 oz) boneless, skinless chicken thighs, each cut into 5 cm (2 in) pieces

pouring (single/light) cream to garnish

dried fenugreek leaves to garnish

salted butter to garnish

Marinade
185 g (6½ oz/¾ cup) plain yoghurt

1 tablespoon ginger paste (page 12)

1 tablespoon garlic paste (page 12)

1 teaspoon chilli powder

1 teaspoon garam masala (page 11)

½ teaspoon freshly ground whole mace

pinch of tandoori colour (See Note)

½–1 teaspoon salt, or to taste

Sauce
4 large ripe tomatoes, chopped

125 g (4½ oz/½ cup) tomato paste (concentrated purée)

½–1 teaspoon salt, or to taste

1 tablespoon sugar

1 teaspoon chilli powder

2 tablespoons dried fenugreek leaves

50 g (1¾ oz) salted butter

60 ml (2 fl oz/¼ cup) pouring (single/light) cream

1 tablespoon ginger paste (page 12)

1 tablespoon garlic paste (page 12)

To make the marinade, mix together the yoghurt, ginger and garlic pastes, chilli powder, garam masala, mace, tandoori colour and salt in a large bowl.

Add the chicken pieces to the marinade and stir to coat well. Cover and put in the refrigerator to marinate for at least 4 hours.

Preheat the oven to 220°C (430°F).

Remove the chicken from the marinade and put in a roasting tin. Cook in the oven for about 15–20 minutes, or until cooked through. Alternatively, preheat a barbecue or chargrill plate to medium. Sear the chicken pieces for about 1 minute on each side, then cook over a medium heat for about 6 minutes, or until cooked through. Take care not to overcook or the chicken will dry out. Set aside.

To make the sauce, mix together the tomato, tomato paste, salt, sugar, chilli powder and fenugreek leaves in a large heavy-based saucepan over a high heat. Bring to a boil, reduce the heat to low, then cover and simmer for 20 minutes.

Remove from the heat and strain the tomato mixture through a mesh strainer into a heatproof bowl. Scrape the side of the strainer for any residue and press down hard with the back of a spoon so that as much of the tomato mixture as possible goes through. Set aside.

Continue making the sauce. In a medium saucepan, heat the butter and cream over a medium heat, stirring frequently. Stir in the ginger and garlic pastes and cook for 5 minutes, stirring occasionally. Add the strained tomato mixture and stir to combine and heat through.

Add the cooked chicken to the sauce and simmer for a further 5 minutes.

Garnish with a swirl of cream, a few fenugreek leaves and a knob of butter, and serve.

Note: *Tandoori colour is an Indian food colouring that has no taste. You can buy it in Indian grocery stores.*

Dum Ka Murgh

Serves 4

This is a steamed Indian chicken pot roast that is a specialty of Hyderabad. Dum ka murgh essentially means 'cooking under steam'. This cooking style was made popular in India during the fourteenth century. Very slow cooking on a very, very low heat produces a special flavour and keeps the meat plump. The pot is sealed with dough to prevent any moisture or flavour from escaping, and the dish retains all the juices and aromas of its ingredients. Serve with Pulao Rice (page 167).

1 x 1 kg (2 lb 3 oz) chicken

30 g (1 oz) ghee (page 13) or salted butter

2 tablespoons julienned fresh ginger

2 garlic cloves, thinly sliced

2 x 2.5 cm (1 in) cinnamon sticks

4 green cardamom pods

4 black cardamom pods

6 cloves

4 black peppercorns

1 teaspoon whole mace

30 g (1 oz/⅛ cup) sultanas (golden raisins)

150 g (5½ oz/1 cup) Fried Onions (page 209)

Marinade

250 g (9 oz/1 cup) plain yoghurt

½–1 teaspoon salt, or to taste

2 tablespoons finely chopped mint leaves

2 tablespoons finely chopped coriander (cilantro) leaves

4 green chillies, slit to just below the stalk area, top and seeds left intact

Dough for Sealing

200 g (7 oz) atta flour or plain (all-purpose) flour

Joint or cut the chicken into eight serving pieces with a very sharp knife or a cleaver. To do this, remove the legs from the breast section and divide each leg into two pieces – the thigh and the drumstick. Halve the breast section lengthwise along the breastbone, then cut crosswise in half again.

To make the marinade, mix together the ingredients in a large bowl. Add the chicken pieces to the marinade and stir to coat well. Cover and put in the refrigerator to marinate for 30 minutes.

To make the dough for sealing, put the atta or plain flour in a medium bowl and make a well in the centre. Gradually pour in 60–125 ml (2–4 fl oz/¼–½ cup) water while working in the flour, adding a little more water if necessary to form a soft dough. Turn out onto a lightly floured work surface and knead for 5 minutes. Rest for 20 minutes.

Meanwhile, preheat the oven to 120°C (250°F).

Heat the ghee or butter in a frying pan over a medium heat. Add the ginger, garlic, cinnamon, green and black cardamom pods, cloves, peppercorns, mace and sultanas and cook, stirring, for 2 minutes.

Tip this mixture into the bowl containing the chicken and marinade. Add the fried onions and stir to combine thoroughly, then transfer the contents of the bowl to a casserole dish.

Roll out the rested dough so that it is slightly larger in diameter than the opening of the casserole dish. Lay the dough over the top of the casserole dish and seal completely, so that it forms a flour dough lid.

Cook in the oven for at least 2 hours. If you have the time, you can cook this dish for up to 4 hours, as the flavour is improved by longer cooking. However, you should reduce the oven temperature to 100°C (210°F) for the final hour of cooking.

Remove the casserole dish from the oven and rest for 15 minutes. Crack open the dough lid and discard just before serving.

Chicken Moilee

Serves 4

Chicken moilee is a really easy, delicate recipe from Kerala, with poppy seeds and coconut imparting a lovely creaminess to the dish. Serve on a banana leaf for an authentic feel, with just-cooked fluffy white rice (see page 14) and Green Bean Thoran (page 58) – the perfect foils for its subtle flavours.

2 tablespoons vegetable or canola oil

1 onion, chopped

1 kg (2 lb 3 oz) boneless, skinless chicken thighs, each cut into 3 cm (1¼ in) pieces

1 tablespoon ground cumin

1 teaspoon turmeric

1 tablespoon ginger paste (page 12)

1 tablespoon garlic paste (page 12)

1 tablespoon poppy seeds, ground

2.5 cm (1 in) cinnamon stick

½ teaspoon black peppercorns

3–4 green chillies, slit to just below the stalk area, top and seeds left intact

1 tomato, chopped

250 ml (8½ fl oz/1 cup) fresh coconut milk (page 14) or canned coconut milk

½–1 teaspoon salt, or to taste

Heat the oil in a large heavy-based saucepan over a medium heat. Sauté the onion, stirring occasionally, for about 5 minutes, or until translucent.

Stir in the chicken, cumin, turmeric, ginger and garlic pastes, poppy seeds, cinnamon, peppercorns, chillies, tomato, coconut milk and salt. Reduce the heat to low, cover and simmer for about 30 minutes, or until the chicken is tender. Serve hot.

Duck Mappas

Serves 4

I first tried this dish on the road from Chennai to Pondicherry in South India, in a little French-settled town where café au lait and pain au chocolat were – and apparently still are – served at the local cafés and restaurants. Forty-two years later, my taste buds can still recall the rich duck flavour, mellowed by the coconut and lifted by the spice combination, with the duck's inherent richness cut through by the acidity of the vinegar. Serve this dish with steamed basmati or other long-grain rice (see page 14).

1 x 1 kg (2 lb 3 oz) organic duck

½–1 teaspoon salt, or to taste

½ teaspoon black peppercorns, crushed

Sauce

60 g (2 oz) ghee (page 13) or 60 ml (2 fl oz/¼ cup) vegetable or canola oil

2 onions, chopped

1 tablespoon chilli powder

2 tablespoons ground coriander

1 teaspoon turmeric

250 ml (8½ fl oz/1 cup) fresh coconut milk (page 14) or canned coconut milk

1 tablespoon white vinegar

Tempering

30 g (1 oz) ghee (page 13) or salted butter

2.5 cm (1 in) cinnamon stick, ground

3 cloves

1 teaspoon black mustard seeds

Preheat the oven to 180°C (350°F).

Put the duck in a roasting tin, sprinkle with the salt and pepper and pour in 125 ml (4 fl oz/½ cup) water around the duck. Cook in the oven for about 1¼ hours, or until tender. Remove from the oven and leave to cool a little.

While the duck is cooking, make the sauce. Heat the ghee or oil in a large frying pan or saucepan. Sauté the onions, stirring occasionally, for about 5 minutes, or until translucent. Stir in the chilli powder, coriander and turmeric and cook for about 1 minute. Stir in the coconut milk and vinegar, reduce the heat to low and cook uncovered for 10 minutes. Set aside.

When the duck is cool enough to handle, joint or cut it into eight serving pieces with a very sharp knife or a cleaver. To do this, remove the legs from the breast section and divide each leg into two pieces – the thigh and drumstick. Halve the breast section lengthwise along the breastbone, then cut crosswise in half again.

Add the cooked duck and the roasting juices from the roasting tin to the sauce in the pan and cook over a low heat for 10 minutes.

To make the tempering, heat the ghee or butter over a high heat in a small frying pan. Add the cinnamon, cloves and mustard seeds and heat until the mustard seeds start to crackle.

Remove from the heat immediately, pour over the duck curry and stir through. Serve hot.

MEAT

In ancient India, communities ate and enjoyed all kinds of meat, but as time passed and traditions changed religious, economic and social influences limited the variety of meat consumed. The cow became a holy animal in Hinduism, and most Hindus do not eat beef. Muslims and Jews cannot eat pork, and many Christians and Parsees, out of respect to their Hindu neighbours, stay away from beef as well. The most popular meats consumed are thus lamb, poultry and goat meat. Offal is also popular and many traditional recipes showcase lambs' and goats' brains and livers.

Many Indians prefer to use meat on the bone for cooking, as it can add extra flavour to curries and tandoori dishes – see Roasted Lamb Shank Masala (page 156) and Tandoori-style Lamb Cutlets (page 140). If you do wish to use meat on the bone ask your butcher to cut up lamb or goat forequarters, shoulders or shanks into small 3–4 cm (2¼–2½ in) pieces, or buy a combination of meat on the bone and diced meat from the supermarket. You will be justly rewarded with the result.

Other, less-used cuts of meat in Indian cooking include pork chops, belly and ribs, as well as pork neck and leg, veal or osso bucco. Venison is sometimes used as it responds well to spice cooking. Minced (ground) meat is used extensively in Indian cuisine.

The dishes in this chapter each have their own individual flavours and characteristics, and have much more variety in heat, texture and taste compared to the curries served in most Indian takeaway restaurants. Explore these recipes, match them to other dishes in this book and create an Indian banquet of your very own!

Lamb Roganjosh

Serves 4

Roganjosh is a mainstay of Indian restaurants and takeaways. The word rogan refers to the red oil or glaze that develops on top of the curry as it cooks, while josh means 'something pleasing that packs a punch'. Originally from Kashmir, the traditional recipe did not include onions or tomatoes. The roganjosh most people are familiar with is a North Indian version with the sweet flavour of caramelised onion, ginger and tomato. This recipe is a simplified version, which is just as delicious using meat on or off the bone. Serve with Pulao Rice (page 167) or Naan (page 200), Parathas (page 206) or Masala Pappadums (page 22).

60 ml (2 fl oz/¼ cup) vegetable or canola oil

6 green cardamom pods

2 large onions, sliced

1 tablespoon ginger paste (page 12)

2 tablespoons garlic paste (page 12)

250 g (9 oz/1 cup) plain yoghurt

2 teaspoons turmeric

2 teaspoons chilli powder

1 kg (2 lb 3 oz) diced lamb or 1 kg (2 lb 3 oz) lamb chops, or a combination of both (see Note)

½–1 teaspoon salt, or to taste

2 tablespoons tomato paste (concentrated purée)

Heat the oil in a large heavy-based saucepan over a medium heat. Add the cardamom pods and onion and sauté, stirring occasionally, for 5–7 minutes, or until well browned. Stir in the ginger and garlic pastes and cook for a further 2 minutes.

Stir in the yoghurt, turmeric and chilli powder, then add the lamb and salt with 60 ml (2 fl oz/¼ cup) water. Stir, then cover and simmer for about 1 hour, or until the meat is tender, adding a little more water if required to keep the curry moist.

Stir in the tomato paste, reduce the heat to low, cover again and cook for a further 20 minutes, or until the meat is fall-apart tender. Serve hot.

Note: You can use diced lamb, which is boneless, or you can choose from lamb forequarter or shoulder chops, slices of lamb shank or marrow bones. Get your butcher to cut shoulder chops and marrow bones into 3 cm (1¼ in) pieces. Traditionally, Indian cooks use a combination of meat cut both on and off the bone.

Tandoori-style Lamb Cutlets

Serves 4

Grilling (broiling) or barbecuing meat and vegetables over charcoal is a really important method in Indian cooking. It is done in a clay oven, the tandoor, or in a sigri, an open steel grate with a charcoal fire. The sigri technique can be more easily replicated at home with a Western-style barbecue. If you use charcoal, you will be richly rewarded with fantastic flavours. Gas barbecues or chargrill pans are the next best alternative. Serve with Naan (page 200) or Parathas (page 206), and a leafy green salad.

12 lamb cutlets or 2 x 8-bone racks of lamb (see Note)

Green Chutney (page 188) to serve

Onion Salad (page 180) to serve

lime wedges to serve

Marinade
2 teaspoons chilli powder

1 teaspoon ground cumin

1 teaspoon ground coriander

1 teaspoon turmeric

½–1 teaspoon salt, or to taste

2 tablespoons mustard oil or vegetable or canola oil

2 tablespoons white vinegar

125 g (4½ oz/½ cup) plain yoghurt

If you are using the racks of lamb, cut each rack into 4 x 2-bone portions. Using a very sharp knife, remove one bone completely from each portion and scrape away the meat and fat at the top of the remaining bone to provide a clean 'handle'. Alternatively, ask your butcher to do this for you.

To make the marinade, mix together the chilli powder, cumin, coriander, turmeric, salt, oil and vinegar in a large shallow bowl. Add the lamb cutlets to the marinade and coat well. Cover and put in the refrigerator to marinate for 1 hour.

Stir the yoghurt through the marinade, making sure it is mixed thoroughly and coats the lamb. Refrigerate for a further 1 hour.

Preheat a barbecue, chargrill pan or grill (broiler) to a high heat. Remove the lamb from the marinade and barbecue or grill on one side until sealed and seared – about 2 minutes for the thin cutlets, and about 4 minutes if you are using the thick, 'double' cutlets. Turn the cutlets over and cook for a further 2 minutes for thin cutlets, and a further 4 minutes for thick cutlets. The cutlets are ready when they are seared on the outside but pink and juicy inside.

Serve with green chutney, onion salad and lime wedges for squeezing over.

Note: Lamb cutlets are the individually separated rib chops from a rack of lamb. They are almost always sold by butchers already French-trimmed, which means that the meat and fat at the top of the bone have been scraped away using a very sharp knife to provide a clean 'handle'. If you are using the racks of lamb for this recipe, you could ask your butcher to prepare the racks into the 4 x 2-bone portions described instead of doing it yourself.

Lamb Kata Masala

Serves 4

Not every curry has to be rich or complicated. Of all the curries that I remember from my childhood, this easy North Indian home-style recipe would have to be the most popular. It is a special favourite with young children who enjoy mopping it up with fresh bread, using their fingers of course! It uses the bhunao cooking technique, which is constant stir-frying over a high heat for 20 minutes or more until the meat and spices have a roasted, toasted taste. Serve this dish with steamed basmati or other long-grain rice (see page 14) or home-style Indian breads such as Missie Roti (page 205) or Parathas (page 206).

1 kg (2 lb 3 oz) diced lamb or 1 kg (2 lb 3 oz) lamb chops, or a combination of both (see Note on page 138)

2 large onions, sliced

2 tablespoons chopped fresh ginger

2 tablespoons chopped garlic

1 teaspoon chilli powder

1 teaspoon turmeric

4 green cardamom pods

4 cloves

4 black peppercorns

2.5 cm (1 in) cinnamon stick

2 tablespoons vegetable or canola oil

4 large tomatoes, chopped, or 400 g (14 oz) can diced tomatoes, drained

125 g (4½ oz/½ cup) plain yoghurt

½–1 teaspoon salt, or to taste

coriander (cilantro) leaves to garnish

Mix together the lamb, onion, ginger, garlic, chilli powder, turmeric, cardamom pods, cloves, peppercorns, cinnamon, oil, tomato, yoghurt and salt in a large heavy-based saucepan over a medium heat. Bring to a boil.

When it just starts to bubble, reduce the heat to low, cover and cook for at least 1 hour, or until the lamb is fall-apart tender, adding 60 ml (2 fl oz/¼ cup) water if required to keep it moist.

Remove the lid, increase the heat to high and bhunao (stir-fry) over a high heat for about 15 minutes, until most of the liquid has evaporated and the oil separates from the meat.

Stir in 125 ml (4 fl oz/½ cup) water to form a thick sauce, garnish with the coriander and serve hot.

Hara keema with Spinach and Mint

Serves 4

Minced (ground) meat is a popular ingredient in Indian cooking. I certainly love using it because of its versatility – koftas, kababs, Indian-style pâtés and simple curries are just the tip of the huge collection of Indian minced meat recipes. This green curry – hara means 'green' in Hindi – has a delicious fresh tang, and it can be cooked and ready to serve in 30 minutes. Eat it with Pooris (page 204), Parathas (page 206) or Chapattis (page 202).

200 g (7 oz) English spinach, washed thoroughly and roughly chopped

2 tablespoons mint leaves

1 tablespoon coriander (cilantro) leaves

2 tablespoons vegetable or canola oil

2 green cardamom pods

2.5 cm (1 in) cinnamon stick

4 cloves

1 tablespoon ginger paste (page 12)

1 tablespoon garlic paste (page 12)

1 small onion, chopped

3 green chillies, chopped

750 g (1 lb 11 oz) minced (ground) beef, lamb or goat

½–1 teaspoon salt, or to taste

½ teaspoon ground white pepper

185 g (6½ oz/¾ cup) plain yoghurt

½ teaspoon garam masala (page 11)

Blanch the spinach in a large saucepan of boiling water for 2 minutes. Drain, allow to cool a little, then transfer to a food processor. Add the mint and coriander leaves and process to a purée. Set aside.

Heat the oil in a large heavy-based saucepan over a medium heat. Add the cardamom pods, cinnamon and cloves and heat until they begin to crackle. Immediately add the ginger and garlic pastes and cook, stirring continuously, for about 1 minute. Add the onion and chilli and sauté, stirring occasionally, for about 4 minutes, or until the onion is golden brown.

Add the meat, salt and white pepper, and stir to mix together and break up the meat with the back of the spoon so that it separates rather than clumping together. Sauté over a medium heat, stirring occasionally, for about 15 minutes, or until the meat is browned.

Stir in the yoghurt and cook over a medium heat for 5 minutes, or until the mixture is almost dry. Stir in the reserved spinach purée and heat through.

Sprinkle over the garam masala and stir through, then serve hot.

Lamb Korma

Serves 4

Kormas are mild, rich curries that have many diverse ingredients and may vary in colour and taste. Think of the great Mughal kings and their dancing girls, music, poetry, statesmanship – do not let your mind dwell on average takeaways. This wonderful recipe must be treated with respect, cooked in a leisurely fashion, and served with Pulao Rice (page 167) or Chapattis (page 202), Naan (page 200) or Parathas (page 206) to accompany it.

125 g (4½ oz/½ cup) plain yoghurt

½–1 teaspoon salt, or to taste

1 kg (2 lb 3 oz) diced lamb or 1 kg (2 lb 3 oz) lamb chops, or a combination of both (see Note on page 138)

30 g (1 oz) ghee (page 13) or 2 tablespoons vegetable or canola oil (see Notes)

4 green cardamom pods

1 teaspoon whole mace

1 whole dried red chilli

1 large onion, chopped

2 teaspoons ginger paste (page 12)

2 teaspoons garlic paste (page 12)

1½ tablespoons ground coriander

¼ teaspoon turmeric

55 g (2 oz/½ cup) ground almonds

125 ml (4 fl oz/½ cup) pouring (single/light) cream

¼ teaspoon saffron infusion (page 13)

1 tablespoon white poppy seeds, ground

small handful chopped dried apricots, sunflower seeds, cashew nuts and sultanas (golden raisins) to garnish (see Notes)

pouring (single/light) cream to garnish

In a large bowl, mix together the yoghurt and salt. Add the lamb and stir to coat with the mixture, then marinate in the refrigerator for 2 hours.

Heat the ghee or oil in a large heavy-based saucepan over a medium heat. Add the cardamom pods, mace and chilli and cook for 30 seconds. Add the onion and sauté, stirring occasionally, for about 5 minutes, or until translucent.

Add the ginger and garlic pastes, coriander and turmeric and stir to mix through. Stir in the lamb with the marinating yoghurt, then cover, reduce the heat to low and cook for about 1½ hours, or until the meat is almost tender.

Stir the ground almonds, cream, saffron infusion and poppy seeds through the korma. Cover, reduce the heat to very low and simmer for a further 20 minutes, or until the lamb is melt-in-the-mouth tender.

Garnish with the dried apricots, sunflower seeds, cashew nuts and sultanas, and a swirl of cream.

Notes: Ghee really is preferable for this recipe. You could replace it with oil, but be aware that the final flavour will not be as rich and subtle.

The dried fruit, seed and nut mix will keep well in an airtight container, and can be used to garnish other curries.

Apricot Lamb Curry

Serves 4

Amidst all the hot and spicy meat recipes from the Mumbai and Goan regions, here is a lovely, delicate Persian-influenced recipe from West India, especially good for when you lack preparation time. The sweet and tart taste of dried apricots cuts through the richness of the lamb. For the very best results, use milk-fed lamb (unweaned lamb, which is usually between four and six weeks old) and serve with steamed basmati or other long-grain rice (see page 14).

1 kg (2 lb 3 oz) diced lamb or 1 kg (2 lb 3 oz) lamb shoulder or forequarter chops, or a combination of both (see Note on page 138)

2 large onions, chopped

1 tablespoon chopped fresh ginger

1 tablespoon chopped garlic

3 large whole dried red chillies

90 g (3 oz/½ cup) dried apricots

5 green cardamom pods

2 black cardamom pods

4 cloves

7.5 cm (3 in) cinnamon stick

250 g (9 oz/1 cup) plain yoghurt

1 tablespoon sugar

½–1 teaspoon salt, or to taste

Put the lamb, onion, ginger, garlic, chillies, apricots, green and black cardamom pods, cloves, cinnamon, yoghurt, sugar and salt in a large heavy-based saucepan. Mix together, then cover the saucepan and bring to a boil over a medium heat, stirring occasionally.

Reduce the heat to low and simmer, covered, for about 1 hour, or until almost all the moisture has evaporated and the meat is fall-apart tender.

Increase the heat to medium and bhunao (stir-fry) the curry for about 20 minutes, until the oil separates from the spices and a glaze forms on the meat. The meat should be really tender by now, with a glossy golden hue. Serve hot.

Dal Mein Gosht

Serves 4

Dal mein gosht is a traditional meat and lentil curry, with meat that is fall-apart tender in a comforting thick lentil sauce. Rainy days and this recipe just go together. Add some Tomato Chutney (page 194), a bowl of just-cooked basmati or other long-grain rice (see page 14), drizzle with hot ghee, and forget the world outside.

60 ml (2 fl oz/¼ cup) vegetable or canola oil

2 bay leaves

5 cm (2 in) cinnamon stick

4 cloves

4 green cardamom pods

1 small onion, chopped

1 teaspoon chilli powder

1 teaspoon turmeric

1 tablespoon coriander seeds, roasted and ground (page 10)

1 tablespoon cumin seeds, roasted and ground (page 10)

2 teaspoons ginger paste (page 12)

2 teaspoons garlic paste (page 12)

1 kg (2 lb 3 oz) diced beef, lamb or goat or 1 kg (2 lb 3 oz) beef, lamb or goat chops, or a combination of both (see Note)

110 g (4 oz/½ cup) split yellow peas, washed and drained

½–1 teaspoon salt, or to taste

chopped coriander (cilantro) leaves to garnish

Heat the oil in a large heavy-based saucepan over a medium heat. Stir in the bay leaves, cinnamon, cloves, cardamom pods and onion and cook, stirring occasionally, for 5–7 minutes, or until the onion is brown.

Meanwhile, mix together the chilli powder, turmeric, ground coriander and cumin with 125 ml (4 fl oz/½ cup) water in a small bowl to make a paste. Set aside.

Add the ginger and garlic pastes to the saucepan and cook, stirring, for 30 seconds. Add the reserved spice paste and cook, stirring, for 30 seconds.

Add the meat, split yellow peas and salt and stir to coat with the spices. Add 750 ml (25½ fl oz/3 cups) water and salt, and bring to a boil.

Reduce the heat to low, cover and simmer for about 1½ hours, or until the meat is beautifully tender, the split yellow peas are soft and the sauce is thick. Check regularly during the cooking period to see if the liquid has evaporated and the curry is drying out. If it is, add water, 125 ml (4 fl oz/½ cup) at a time, to keep it moist.

Garnish with the chopped coriander and serve.

Note: You can use diced meat, which is boneless, or you could choose from lamb or goat forequarter or shoulder chops, slices of lamb shank, beef shank or veal shank (the cut of meat used for osso bucco), or beef cheek or beef, lamb or goat marrow bones. Get your butcher to cut shoulder chops and marrow bones into 3 cm (1¼ in) pieces.

Meat Patiala

Serves 4

Punjab is well known for its robust, spicy curries, bursting with flavour and rich in ghee. Enjoy this recipe from Patiala, in south-eastern Punjab, and use either lamb or goat forequarter or shoulder chops, or slices of lamb shank, beef shank or veal shank (the cut of meat used for osso bucco) to add fantastic texture and flavour. Cutting the meat on the bone adds more flavour – your butcher can do this for you. Serve the curry with Parathas (page 206) or Chapattis (page 202).

125 g (4½ oz) ghee (page 13)
or 125 ml (4 fl oz/½ cup)
vegetable or canola oil

1 kg (2 lb 3 oz) diced beef, lamb
or goat or 1 kg (2 lb 3 oz)
beef, lamb or goat chops, or
a combination of both (see
Note on page 148)

2 onions, chopped

½–1 teaspoon salt, or to taste

2 tablespoons ginger paste
(page 12)

2 tablespoons garlic paste
(page 12)

4 black cardamom pods

5 cloves

2 bay leaves

2 x 2.5 cm (1 in) cinnamon
sticks

1 teaspoon black peppercorns

2 teaspoons chilli powder

1 teaspoon turmeric

2 tablespoons ground coriander

2 tomatoes, chopped

2 tablespoons sliced fresh
ginger

2 tablespoons cumin seeds,
roasted and ground
(page 10)

chopped coriander (cilantro)
leaves to garnish

Heat the ghee or oil in a large heavy-based saucepan over a medium heat. Add the meat, onion and salt and cook, stirring occasionally, for about 15–20 minutes, or until the meat is browned.

Stir in the ginger and garlic pastes and sauté, stirring occasionally, for 8–10 minutes.

Stir in the cardamom pods, cloves, bay leaves, cinnamon and peppercorns. There should be enough moisture for the onion and spices to coat the meat. If the ingredients are sticking to the base of the pan, stir in up to 250 ml (8½ fl oz/1 cup) water. Reduce the heat to low, cover and simmer for about 1 hour, or until the meat is almost cooked.

Stir in the chilli powder and turmeric and cook for 30 seconds, then add the ground coriander. Increase the heat to high, stir in the tomato and cook until it disintegrates and forms a smooth sauce.

Stir in the ginger and cumin, then garnish with plenty of chopped coriander and serve.

149

Bhuna Gosht

Serves 4

The British called all the dishes they encountered in India 'curry'. However, every curry is cooked with a distinctive technique that results in a special flavour and texture. This family favourite, a North Indian recipe, is a fairly dry curry – its individual flavour obtained by constant bhunao-ing (stir-frying) until the meat and spices have a roasted, toasted taste. Serve it with Pooris (page 204), Parathas (page 206) or steamed basmati rice (see page 14).

60 ml (2 fl oz/¼ cup) vegetable or canola oil

2 large onions, chopped

2 tablespoons ginger paste (page 12)

2 tablespoons garlic paste (page 12)

2 tablespoons cumin seeds, roasted and ground (page 10)

3 tablespoons coriander seeds, roasted and ground (page 10)

1 teaspoon fenugreek seeds, roasted and ground (page 10)

2 teaspoons turmeric

2 teaspoons chilli powder

60 g (2 oz/¼ cup) plain yoghurt

1 kg (2 lb 3 oz) diced beef, lamb or goat or 1 kg (2 lb 3 oz) beef, lamb or goat chops, or a combination of both (see Note on page 148)

½–1 teaspoon salt, or to taste

coriander (cilantro) leaves to garnish

Heat the oil in a large heavy-based saucepan over a medium heat. Sauté the onion, stirring occasionally, for about 10 minutes, or until dark brown. Add the ginger and garlic pastes and sauté, stirring frequently, for 2 minutes.

Mix together the cumin, coriander, fenugreek, turmeric and chilli powder in a small bowl. Tip this into the onion mixture and cook, stirring continuously, for 2 minutes, while gradually adding the yoghurt at the same time to moisten the mixture and prevent it from sticking.

Add the meat and salt and stir to mix through. Increase the heat to high and stir-fry over a high heat for about 20 minutes, or until the oil separates from the masala (the combination of spices) and a glaze or shine develops on the meat.

Stir in 250 ml (8½ fl oz/1 cup) water, then reduce the heat to low, cover and simmer for about 40 minutes, or until the meat is tender.

Garnish with plenty of coriander leaves and serve.

Lamb Pasanda Hariyali

Serves 4

Most Indian meat curries are cooked on the bone for the added concentrated flavour that it gives to the meat. But there are some exceptions. Pasanda (from the word pasand, which means 'liked by everyone') is a special, tender cut of meat – lamb or goat is used in India – that is usually taken from the top of the leg and flattened. However, this recipe uses the backstrap of lamb or lamb loin fillets – thin but extra-tender cuts of meat. Once the 4–8 hours of marinating is done, this really is a very quick, fresh-tasting dish to make. Serve it with Naan (page 200), Chapattis (page 202) or Parathas (page 206) and a Raita (pages 198–199).

800 g (1 lb 12 oz) lamb backstraps or lamb loin fillet

1 tablespoon vegetable or canola oil

30 g (1 oz) ghee (page 13) or 2 tablespoons vegetable or canola oil

1 onion, sliced

sliced red chilli to garnish

lemon or lime wedges dipped in crushed chillies to garnish (see Note)

Green Masala

200 g (7 oz) English spinach, washed thoroughly and roughly chopped

4 spring onions (scallions), roughly chopped

1 tablespoon chopped fresh ginger

1 tablespoon chopped garlic

1½ tablespoons sesame seeds, coarsely ground

½–1 teaspoon salt, or to taste

4 green chillies

small handful mint leaves

large handful coriander (cilantro) leaves

To make the green masala, blanch the spinach in a large saucepan of boiling water for 2 minutes. Drain, allow to cool a little, then transfer to a food processor. Add the spring onion, ginger, garlic, sesame seeds, salt, chillies, mint and coriander and process to make a smooth purée.

Clean the lamb backstraps or lamb loin fillets. Cut each backstrap or fillet into eight pieces, then flatten to about 1 cm (½ in) thick with a meat mallet or the flat edge of a large knife or cleaver. Put the lamb in a shallow dish and coat thoroughly with the green masala. Cover and put in the refrigerator to marinate for 4–8 hours.

Heat 1 tablespoon of the oil in a large frying pan over a high heat. Add the lamb with the marinade and cook for 1 minute on each side to seal the meat.

Reduce the heat to low. Put a metal plate slightly smaller than the frying pan on top of the meat and weigh it down with something heavy (such as food cans) to stop the meat from curling up. Cook for a further 5–7 minutes. Remove from the heat and rest the lamb for 5 minutes.

Meawhile, in a separate large frying pan, heat the ghee or oil over a high heat. Add the onion, reduce the heat to medium and sauté for about 8 minutes, or until golden brown.

Mix the onion with the rested lamb to combine thoroughly, then serve immediately garnished with sliced red chilli and lemon wedges.

Note: To make the garnish, using a mortar and pestle grind 1 tablespoon of crushed chillies to a coarse powder. Transfer to a plate and dip the lemon or lime wedges in the powder to coat them. The wedges will absorb a little of the heat from the chillies and add an extra kick when squeezed over the lamb.

Lamb Biryani

Serves 4–6

There are many recipes for lamb biryani, India's favourite lamb and rice dish, served from street cafés, at school fairs and at weddings. This is a really easy recipe that comes from 'hole-in-the-wall' restaurants in old Delhi. It all depends on the rich flavour of the lamb stock. This is a perfect example of the fantastic flavour and gelatinous texture that the secondary cuts of lamb can give to a dish. Serve it with Cucumber Raita (page 198).

60 g (2 oz) ghee (page 13) or 60 ml (2 fl oz/¼ cup) vegetable or canola oil

4 green cardamom pods

6 cm (2½ in) cinnamon stick

4 green chillies, slit to just below the stalk area, top and seeds left intact

500 g (1 lb 2 oz/2½ cups) basmati rice or other long-grain rice, washed and drained

60 g (2 oz/¼ cup) plain yoghurt

1 tablespoon saffron infusion (page 13)

½–1 teaspoon salt, or to taste

½ teaspoon turmeric

3–4 drops of kewra water (optional) (see Note on page 156)

unsalted roasted cashew nuts to garnish

sultanas (golden raisins) to garnish

Lamb and Stock

30 g (1 oz) ghee (page 13) or 2 tablespoons mustard oil

6 green cardamom pods

4 black cardamom pods

½ teaspoon whole mace

4 cm (1½ in) cinnamon stick

4 green chillies, slit to just below the stalk area, top and seeds left intact

1 tablespoon ginger paste (page 12)

1 tablespoon garlic paste (page 12)

1 kg (2 lb 3 oz) lamb on the bone, such as rib chops, shoulder chops, spare ribs and marrow bones (see Note)

250 g (9 oz /1 cup) plain yoghurt

½–1 teaspoon salt, or to taste

To prepare the lamb and stock, heat the ghee or mustard oil in a large heavy-based saucepan over a medium heat. If you are using mustard oil, heat it until it is smoking. Add the green and black cardamom pods, mace, cinnamon and chillies and heat until the spices begin to crackle. Stir in the ginger and garlic pastes and cook for 2 minutes.

Stir in the lamb, yoghurt and salt. Add about 1 litre (34 fl oz/4 cups) water and bring to a boil, then cover and simmer for about 1 hour, or until the meat is tender.

In a separate large heavy-based saucepan, heat the ghee or oil over a medium heat. Add the green cardamom pods, cinnamon, chillies and rice and sauté, stirring continuously, until the ghee or oil coats every grain of rice.

Add the cooked lamb and 750 ml (25½ fl oz/3 cups) of the cooking stock and stir to mix through. (If the stock has been reduced to less than 750 ml, add enough water to make it up to this quantity.)

Stir in the yoghurt, saffron infusion and salt. Bring to a boil, then reduce the heat to as low as possible, cover and cook for about 20 minutes, or until almost all the stock is absorbed.

Mix together the turmeric and 1 tablespoon water in a small bowl until dissolved, then carefully pour it in one place on top of the almost-cooked rice, but do not stir. Cover and continue cooking for about 15 minutes, or until all the liquid is absorbed and the rice is cooked.

If you wish, gently stir the biryani just before serving – this is done to produce the trademark yellow and white grains of a biryani, but you must do it very carefully to avoid breaking up the rice grains.

Sprinkle with the kewra water, if using, garnish with cashew nuts and sultanas and serve.

Note: Ask your butcher to cut shoulder chops and marrow bones into 3 cm (1¼ in) pieces.

Meat Kolhapuri

Serves 4

This is a very spicy hot red meat curry from Kolhapur in western India – reduce the chilli if you would like a medium–hot version. I came across this recipe when I worked in Mumbai during the 1980s. It was quite a shock to my tame North-East Indian palate – and is a winner at the Spice Kitchen with all the macho male diners. Serve with plenty of steamed basmati or other long-grain rice (see page 14).

1 kg (2 lb 3 oz) diced beef, lamb or goat or 1 kg (2 lb 3 oz) beef, lamb or goat chops, or a combination of both (see Note on page 148)

2 tablespoons vegetable or canola oil

3 large potatoes, peeled and halved

8 cloves, ground

8 black peppercorns, ground

2 tablespoons poppy seeds, finely ground

1 tablespoon coriander seeds, ground

1 tablespoon fennel seeds, ground

1–2 tablespoons chilli powder, to taste

small handful coriander (cilantro) leaves, chopped, to garnish

Marinade
½–2 teaspoons salt, or to taste

2 teaspoons turmeric

1 tablespoon ginger paste (page 12)

1 tablespoon garlic paste (page 12)

Onion and Tomato Paste
2 tablespoons vegetable or canola oil

3 large onions, chopped

45 g (1½ oz/½ cup) desiccated (grated dried) coconut

2 tomatoes, chopped

To make the marinade, mix together the salt, turmeric and ginger and garlic pastes in a large bowl. Add the meat and stir to coat thoroughly, then cover and put in the refrigerator to marinate for 1 hour.

To make the onion and tomato paste, heat the oil in a large heavy-based saucepan over a medium heat. Sauté the onion, stirring occasionally, for about 5 minutes, or until brown. Stir in the coconut and tomato and cook for about 2 minutes. Remove from the heat and allow to cool a little, then transfer the mixture to a food processor and process to a paste. Set aside.

Heat the oil in the same saucepan over a high heat. Add the meat with its marinade and the potatoes, and stir-fry for about 8 minutes, or until well browned.

Reduce the heat to medium. Stir in the ground cloves, black pepper, ground poppy seeds, ground coriander and fennel, chilli powder, the reserved onion and tomato paste and 250 ml (8½ fl oz/1 cup) water. Cover and cook for about 45 minutes, or until the meat is tender.

Garnish with the coriander leaves and serve hot.

Roasted Lamb Shank Masala

Serves 4

This is a lovely, rich, fall-apart-tender lamb shank recipe for very cold days. At the Spice Kitchen we roast the shanks in the tandoor before finishing the recipe by simmering them in the sauce. The wonderful charcoal aromas cannot be duplicated in a conventional oven, but you could use a barbecue or chargrill pan if you really wanted to get as close as possible to those smells and flavours. Serve with plenty of Chapattis (page 202) or Naan (page 200) and Pulao Rice (page 167), plus a Spinach Raita (page 198) or leafy green salad to finish off this delectable dish.

1 kg (2 lb 3 oz) lamb shanks

250 g (9 oz/1 cup) plain yoghurt

½–1 teaspoon salt, or to taste

½ teaspoon mace flakes

1 tablespoon cumin seeds

1 tablespoon coriander seeds

1 teaspoon fenugreek seeds

60 ml (2 fl oz/¼ cup) vegetable or canola oil

4 cloves

4 black cardamom pods

2 bay leaves

2 large onions, sliced

1 tablespoon ginger paste (page 12)

1 tablespoon garlic paste (page 12)

1 teaspoon chilli powder

2 tablespoons desiccated (grated dried) coconut

1½ tablespoons dark rum

1 tablespoon kewra water (optional) (see Note)

Preheat the oven to 160°C (320°F). Pierce the lamb shanks all over with a fork and put in a shallow dish. In a small bowl, mix together the yoghurt and salt, then coat the lamb shanks with the mixture. Cover and put in the refrigerator to marinate for about 20 minutes.

Transfer the lamb shanks with the marinating yoghurt to a roasting tin, pour in 500 ml (17 fl oz/2 cups) water and roast in the oven for 1–1½ hours, or until cooked.

Meanwhile, grind the mace, cumin, coriander and fenugreek using a mortar and pestle or electric spice grinder until finely ground. Set aside.

About 30 minutes before the lamb shanks have finished roasting, heat the oil in a large frying pan or saucepan over a medium heat. Sauté the cloves, cardamom pods, bay leaves and onion, stirring occasionally, for about 8 minutes, or until the onion is brown. Stir in the ginger and garlic pastes and cook for 1 minute.

Stir in the reserved ground spices, chilli powder and coconut with 190 ml (6½ fl oz/¾ cup) water. Cover and simmer over a medium heat for at least 15 minutes.

Add the roasted lamb shanks and any cooking juices from the roasting tin, as well as the rum and kewra water, if using, to the sauce in the pan. Stir to coat and mix through, then reduce the heat to low, cover and simmer for a further 1 hour.

Remove the saucepan from the heat and rest the lamb shanks for 15 minutes before serving.

Note: Kewra water is extracted from the keora flower and is used to flavour rich Mughal curries and rice dishes. It is less concentrated and lighter in flavour than kewra essence. You can purchase it in Asian and Indian grocery stores. You can omit the kewra water if you do not have any, but its inclusion does add something special to the combination of flavours in this dish.

Pork Belly and Ribs with Curry Leaves, Coconut and Tomato

Serves 4

Pork responds very well to the spice treatment. Its rich flavour is accentuated and cut through at the same time by the pungency of the spices. Slightly acidic flavours such as tomato, tamarind or kokum are often used with pork in Indian cooking. This simple South Indian dish uses fresh chillies, tomatoes, coconut and curry leaves. We serve it at the Spice Kitchen with string hoppers – steamed rice noodle pancakes. You could serve it with steamed basmati or other long-grain rice (see page 14) and a green salad, or with rice noodles.

1 tablespoon ginger paste
(page 12)

1 tablespoon garlic paste
(page 12)

1 tablespoon palm sugar or
dark brown sugar

½–1 teaspoon salt, or to taste

500 g (1 lb 2 oz) pork belly, cut
into 2.5 cm (1 in) pieces

500 g (1 lb 2 oz) pork ribs, cut
into 2.5 cm (1 in) pieces

2 tablespoons vegetable or
canola oil

2 onions, chopped

100 g (3½ oz) fresh coconut
flesh, diced (see Note), or
2 tablespoons desiccated
(grated dried) coconut

20 curry leaves

2 large tomatoes, chopped

4 green chillies, chopped

2 tablespoons chopped
coriander (cilantro) leaves

Preheat the oven to 180°C (350°F).

Mix together the ginger and garlic pastes, sugar and salt in a large bowl. Add the pork belly and ribs and evenly coat with the paste mixture.

Put the pork in a roasting tin and cook in the oven for about 30 minutes, or until tender. Remove from the oven and leave the pork to rest for 20 minutes. Drain off or scoop off any fat and discard.

Heat the oil in a large heavy-based saucepan over a medium heat. Sauté the onion, stirring occasionally, for about 5 minutes, or until golden brown. Add the coconut and cook, stirring, for 2 minutes.

Stir in the curry leaves, tomato, chilli, coriander and roasted pork and cook for 5 minutes, stirring occasionally. Serve hot.

Note: You should have about 1 cup of diced fresh coconut.

Pork Vindaloo

Serves 4

This Portuguese-inspired dish originated in Goa in the sixteenth century, heralding the arrival of the chilli in India with what is one of the hottest dishes in the Indian repertoire. First made almost as a preserved pickle, tiny amounts were eaten with lots of bread or rice. Gradually the amount of chilli has been lessened to transform it into a main course curry, but it can still bring tears to the eyes. It is traditionally made with pork and red wine vinegar, but you can substitute beef, goat, lamb, duck or venison if you prefer. Serve it with steamed basmati rice (see page 14).

1 kg (2 lb 3 oz) diced pork neck

60 ml (2 fl oz/¼ cup) vegetable or canola oil

1 large onion, chopped

½–1 teaspoon salt, or to taste

Marinade

125 ml (4 fl oz/½ cup) red wine vinegar

1 tablespoon freshly ground black pepper

1 tablespoon sugar

8 green cardamom pods

8 cloves

5 green chillies, slit to just below the stalk area, top and seeds left intact

Vindaloo Paste

2½ teaspoons chilli powder

2 x 5 cm (2 in) cinnamon sticks, finely ground

1 tablespoon ground cumin

2 tablespoons turmeric

2 tablespoons ginger paste (page 12)

1 tablespoon garlic paste (page 12)

60 ml (2 fl oz/¼ cup) red wine vinegar

1 tablespoon hot English mustard

To make the marinade, mix together the vinegar, pepper, sugar, cardamom pods, cloves and chillies in a large bowl.

Add the pork and stir to coat thoroughly, then cover and put in the refrigerator to marinate for at least 4 hours.

To make the vindaloo paste, mix together the chilli powder, cinnamon, cumin, turmeric, ginger and garlic pastes, vinegar and mustard in a small bowl.

Heat the oil in a large heavy-based saucepan over a medium heat. Sauté the onion, stirring occasionally, for about 8 minutes, or until brown. Add the vindaloo paste and stir-fry for about 4 minutes, or until the oil separates from the spices.

Add the pork with the marinade and salt to the saucepan, and stir to mix through. If necessary, stir in 60 ml (2 fl oz/¼ cup) water to obtain a thick sauce. Cover and cook over a low heat for about 45 minutes, until the pork is tender. Check every 10–15 minutes during the cooking time and add 60 ml (2 fl oz/¼ cup) water when necessary so the curry does not dry out and the sauce remains thick – you should not need to add more than 250 ml (8½ fl oz/1 cup) water in total. Serve hot.

Kolkata Pork Sausages

Serves 4

A Portuguese-inspired sausage dish, these are a specialty of Entally, a neighbourhood of Kolkata (Calcutta). These spicy sausages are a real hit at breakfast, brunch, lunch or dinner, and once tasted, you will be addicted. You can buy sausage skins from your butcher, and if you have a sausage maker, homemade sausages are easy. This will also ensure that you only use the best cuts of meat in the sausages. If you don't have a sausage maker, you can shape the mixture into patties, which are equally delicious. Serve with steamed rice (see page 14) or mashed potato.

250 g (9 oz) minced (ground) pork belly

50 g (1¾ oz) pork fat, very finely diced

2 onions, finely chopped

2 large handfuls finely chopped mint leaves

2 large handfuls finely chopped coriander (cilantro) leaves

2 tablespoons finely chopped green chilli

1 teaspoon ground cinnamon

2 teaspoons freshly ground black pepper

½–1 teaspoon salt, or to taste

8 sausage skins, from the butcher (optional)

1 tablespoon vegetable or canola oil (optional)

In a large bowl, mix together the pork belly and fat, onion, mint, coriander, chilli, cinnamon, pepper and salt.

If you are using a sausage maker, follow the manufacturer's instructions to attach the skin to the sausage maker, then force the sausage mixture through into the skin to form the sausages.

Alternatively, divide the sausage mixture into eight portions. Dip your hands in warm water and, using the palms of your hands, shape the mixture into patties.

Preheat a grill (broiler) or chargrill pan to medium. Cook the sausages under the grill or on the chargrill pan, turning occasionally, for 20–30 minutes, or until they are cooked through. (They will take a little longer to cook than store-bought sausages.)

If you have made patties, cook them under the grill or on the chargrill pan for 5 minutes, then turn and cook on the other side for 3–5 minutes, or until cooked through.

Alternatively, just cover the bottom of a large frying pan with water and heat over a medium heat. Cook the sausages in the pan, turning occasionally, for 20–30 minutes, or until they are cooked through. Add a little more water to the pan as necessary.

To cook the patties using an alternative method, heat the oil in a large frying pan over a medium heat. Cook the patties for about about 4 minutes, or until browned, then turn and cook on the other side for 4 minutes. Carefully pour in 60 ml (2 fl oz/¼ cup) water, cover with a lid and cook for a further 2 minutes.

Serve the sausages or patties hot.

SIDE
DISHES

By far the most common side dish served with an Indian meal is rice. Steamed or fried, simple or elaborate with multiple ingredients, this humble grain features heavily throughout Indian cuisine.

There are many varieties of rice in India, from 'red' Kerala rice to simple long-grain rice. By far the most important and well-known long-grain rice is basmati. This rice originates from a village of the same name in the Himalayan foothills, and has a lovely elegant slender structure, is very low in starch and the only rice recommended for diabetics because of its low glycaemic index. Basmati rice is readily available in supermarkets or Indian grocery stores. Look on the packet to see the age of the rice – new crops or just-harvested rice should be stored for up to five years to allow the flavours to develop and the starch content to lessen. Try to buy already-aged rice, which has a creamier colour and is generally more expensive. Aged rice will cook without getting gluggy or breaking up and will result in a nicer flavour.

Other side dishes can include lentils, vegetables or salads, and are often accompanied with chutneys to contribute to a larger Indian feast. Vegetable dishes such as Poppy Seed Potatoes (page 176), fruity salads such as Mango and Pineapple Salad (page 179), as well as the traditional Onion Salad (page 180) feature regularly. Finally, dal – a soupy lentil preparation – is probably the most popular comfort food and is served with almost all Indian meals.

Lemon Rice

Serves 4

Rice recipes that use already-cooked rice are popular in South India, and lemon rice is considered a delicacy there. It is a lovely way to use up left-over rice. If freshly cooked, the rice should be at room temperature – stirring the hot tempering through it will heat it up. You can serve it hot on a banana leaf with an assortment of curries or just with yoghurt and pickle. It is also great as a warm or cold salad.

1 teaspoon fenugreek seeds

1 tablespoon split white lentils (white urad dal), washed and drained

1 teaspoon turmeric

225 g (8 oz) cooked basmati rice or other long-grain rice (see page 14), at room temperature (see Notes)

juice of 2 lemons

2 tablespoons vegetable or canola oil

30 g (1 oz) raw cashew nuts

30 g (1 oz) raw peanuts

½–1 teaspoon salt, or to taste

Tempering

20 curry leaves

½ teaspoon black mustard seeds

pinch of asafoetida

1 tablespoon split yellow peas washed and drained

2 red chillies

Heat the fenugreek seeds and split white lentils in a heavy-based frying pan over a medium heat for 1 minute. Allow to cool, then grind finely with the turmeric using a mortar and pestle or an electric spice grinder.

Put the cooked rice in a large bowl and stir through the ground spices and split white lentils and the lemon juice.

Heat the oil over a medium heat in the frying pan. Cook the cashew nuts and peanuts, stirring continuously, for about 2 minutes, or until golden brown. Remove the nuts from the pan, drain on kitchen towels and set aside.

Using the oil in the frying pan, make the tempering: add the curry leaves, mustard seeds, asafoetida, split yellow peas and chillies to the pan and cook, stirring continuously, for 2 minutes, or until the mixture is brown.

Pour the tempering over the rice, add the salt and stir to mix together thoroughly.

Garnish with the reserved cashew nuts and peanuts and serve.

Notes: In South Indian cooking, a contrast in texture is often provided by adding lentils and pulses to cooked vegetables. They are not necessarily cooked until soft. Instead, as with the split yellow peas in this recipe, they are washed and drained, and then quickly fried in hot oil or ghee for 1–2 minutes. This gives them a crunchy texture, and as they are fully cooked, they are fine to eat.

You need 100 g (3½ oz) of uncooked basmati rice to yield 225 g (8 oz) of cooked rice.

Pulao Rice

Serves 4

Pulao, from the Persian word 'pilaf' is the beautiful, fragrant, separated rice that is cooked with subtle spices and eaten throughout India. It is the most popular rice accompaniment to be served at an Indian banquet. You can cook pulao rice on the stovetop or in the oven, and vegetables such as potatoes or peas can be added, too. Serve it with all kinds of meat, fish or vegetable curries.

60 g (2 oz) ghee (page 13) or 60 ml (2 fl oz/¼ cup) vegetable or canola oil

4 green cardamom pods

3 cloves

2.5 cm (1 in) cinnamon stick

200 g (7 oz/1 cup) basmati rice or other long-grain rice, washed and drained (see Note)

½–1 teaspoon salt, or to taste

If using the oven for the final stage of cooking the rice, preheat it to 200°C (400°F).

Heat the ghee or oil in a flameproof casserole dish over a medium heat on the stovetop.

Add the cardamom pods, cloves, cinnamon and rice and stir to mix through and coat every rice grain with the ghee or oil. Pour in 375 ml (12½ fl oz/1½ cups) hot water, then add the salt and stir. Bring to a boil.

Reduce the heat to low, cover and cook the rice on the stovetop for about 20 minutes. Do not uncover or stir to ensure that the rice cooks evenly and does not break up. Remove from the heat and rest, still covered, for 10 minutes before serving. (This allows the rice grains to plump up to their maximum length.)

Alternatively, cover the dish with foil once it has come to the boil, then put in the oven and cook for about 25 minutes. Remove the dish from the oven but do not remove the foil, and rest the rice for 10 minutes before serving.

Note: To steam rice successfully, you must add the correct amount of water in proportion to the rice. For every 200 g (7 oz/1 cup) of rice, add 375 ml (12½ fl oz/1½ cups) water.

Variation: To recreate the yellow rice often found in Indian restaurants and takeaways, follow this recipe but add a pinch of turmeric after you've added the hot water.

Black Peppercorn and Cumin Rice

Serves 4

There is always steamed white rice left over in an Indian home. You can add all kinds of ingredients to make complex dishes, but a really good way to refresh left-over rice is with this simple recipe. It is so popular that steamed rice is often cooked specifically to make this dish in its own right. In the Spice Kitchen we are always surprised at how many people ask specially for it. You can serve it as part of an Indian meal, but it is also delicious with a stew or casserole.

60 g (2 oz) ghee (page 13) or 60 ml (2 fl oz/¼ cup) vegetable or canola oil

1 teaspoon black peppercorns

1 teaspoon cumin seeds

280 g (10 oz/1½ cups) cooked basmati rice or other long-grain rice (see Note and page 14)

½–1 teaspoon salt, or to taste

Heat the ghee or oil in a wok or large frying pan over a medium heat. Add the peppercorns and cumin seeds and cook, stirring occasionally, for about 1 minute.

Stir in the cooked rice and salt and heat through, stirring continuously to break up any lumps of rice, for about 4 minutes. Serve hot.

Note: You will need 125 g (4 oz) of uncooked rice to yield 280 g (10 oz/1½ cups) of cooked rice.

Tomato Pulao Rice

Serves 4

*Of the many, many recipes for pulao rice, this version appeared at the time of the first
Portuguese settlement in India, around the sixteenth century. There were no tomatoes in India
before then. Another distinctive feature of this dish is star anise, which is not commonly used in
Indian cooking. A rosy blush covers this special rice dish. Serve it simply with a delicate korma.*

60 g (2 oz) ghee (page 13)
or 60 ml (2 fl oz/¼ cup)
vegetable or canola oil

2 star anise

4 cloves

2.5 cm (1 in) cinnamon stick

200 g (7 oz/1 cup) basmati rice
or other long-grain rice,
washed and drained

2 garlic cloves, chopped

250 g (9 oz/1 cup) tomato
purée (puréed tomatoes) or
4 tomatoes, skin and seeds
removed, puréed (see Note)

½–1 teaspoon salt, or to taste

1 teaspoon sugar (optional)

1 teaspoon cumin seeds,
roasted and ground
(page 10)

Fried Onions (page 209)
to garnish

Heat the ghee or oil in a shallow heavy-based saucepan over a
high heat. Sauté the star anise, cloves, cinnamon and rice, stirring
continuously, until the ghee or oil coats every rice grain.

Stir in the garlic and 375 ml (12½ fl oz/1½ cups) hot water. Bring
to a boil, then reduce the heat to as low as possible, cover, and
cook for about 15 minutes, or until most of the water is absorbed.

Stir in the tomato purée. Add the salt and the sugar, if desired, if
the tomato purée is very sour. (It is important to add the tomato
only at this stage, otherwise the rice may not cook evenly, as the
acid in the tomato slows down the cooking process.) Cover the
pan again and continue cooking for about 12 minutes, or until all
the liquid is absorbed and the rice is fully cooked.

Sprinkle over the cumin, garnish with the fried onions and
serve hot.

*Note: If you are using whole tomatoes to make the tomato purée, score
a cross in the base of each tomato. Put in a heatproof bowl and cover with
boiling water. Leave for 30 seconds, then transfer to cold water. When
cool enough to handle, peel the skin away, starting from the cross. Cut the
tomato in half, scoop out the seeds with a teaspoon and discard. Process
the tomato flesh in a food processor to form a purée. You should have
250 g (9 oz/1 cup) of purée.*

Rajma Dal

Serves 4

Punjab is India's agricultural bowl. Punjabi cuisine abounds with nourishing and satisfying country-style recipes that use locally grown ingredients such as chickpeas and red kidney beans, wheat and corn flours, homemade ghee and panir cheese. Rajma dal is a Punjabi favourite – this simple dish is satisfying and healthy, full of fibre and protein. You may not have to work a 12-hour day on a farm, but you will certainly get enough energy from this dish, served with rice, to face the world for many hours to come.

225 g (8 oz) dried or 600 g (1 lb 5 oz) canned red kidney beans

60 g (2 oz) ghee (page 13) or 60 ml (2 fl oz/¼ cup) vegetable or canola oil (see Note)

1 teaspoon cumin seeds

1 teaspoon chilli powder

1 tablespoon julienned ginger

1 large onion, sliced

60 g (2 oz/¼ cup) tomato paste (concentrated purée) or 2 vine-ripened tomatoes, chopped

If using dried red kidney beans, soak overnight in a bowl of cold salted water. Drain, then put in a medium saucepan with 1.5 litres (51 fl oz/6 cups) fresh water. Bring to a boil, then reduce the heat to medium and cook uncovered, skimming off the residue as it rises to the surface, for about 2½ hours, or until the beans are really tender – they should break up easily when pressed between your thumb and forefinger. Drain the cooked kidney beans, reserving 375 ml (12½ fl oz/1½ cups) of the cooking liquid. Alternatively, if you are using canned red kidney beans, rinse them well in cold water and drain.

Heat the ghee or oil over a medium heat in a large frying pan. Add the cumin seeds, chilli powder and ginger and heat until they begin to crackle. Add the onion and sauté, stirring occasionally, for about 8 minutes, or until golden brown.

Stir in the tomato paste or chopped tomato with 125 ml (4 fl oz/½ cup) water and simmer gently over a low heat for 10 minutes. Add the cooked kidney beans with the reserved cooking liquid, or the drained canned kidney beans along with 250 ml (8½ fl oz/1 cup) water, and simmer for a further 20 minutes. Serve hot.

Note: Ghee really is preferable for this recipe. You can replace it with oil, but the final flavour will not be as rich.

Masoor Dal Tarkewali

Serves 4

Lentils are an important part of the Indian meal. They are a great leveller and comfort food for both the street dweller and the millionaire in the penthouse. The split red lentils (masoor dal) used in this recipe are similar to the red lentils found in supermarkets – they do not need soaking and are easy to cook. They are also very easy to digest, and in fact, in India the cooking water from split red lentils is cooled and given to babies as a substitute for milk. Eat with steamed rice (see page 14) or homemade Indian bread such as Chapattis (page 202), and accompany with meat and vegetable dishes.

250 g (9 oz/1 cup) split red
    lentils (masoor dal) or red
    lentils, washed and drained

1 teaspoon chopped ginger

1 teaspoon chopped garlic

½ small onion, sliced

1 teaspoon turmeric

½–1 teaspoon salt, or to taste

Tempering
60 g (2 oz) ghee (page 13) or
    salted butter

2 teaspoons cumin seeds

1 onion, sliced

1 whole dried red chilli

pinch of chilli powder

2 tablespoons chopped
    coriander (cilantro) leaves

Put the lentils, ginger, garlic, onion and turmeric, along with 750 ml (25½ fl oz/3 cups) water in a large saucepan and stir to combine. Cook uncovered over a medium heat for about 45 minutes, or until the lentils are well cooked and disintegrating to form a purée. Stir in the salt.

To make the tempering, heat the ghee or butter in a small frying pan over a high heat. Cook the cumin seeds, onion, dried red chilli and chilli powder, stirring occasionally, for about 6–8 minutes, or until the onion is golden brown. Stir in the coriander and cook for 1 minute.

Pour the tempering over the cooked dal and serve immediately.

Sambar Dal

Serves 4

A sambar is a South Indian lentil preparation that usually includes vegetables and is flavoured with tamarind. Almost any vegetable can be used in a sambar, and the tamarind provides tartness and preserves the vitamins of the cooked vegetables. Sambars are eaten either with steamed basmati rice (see page 14) or served with dishes such as Upma (page 48) or Cabbage Bondas (page 36).

125 g (4½ oz/½ cup) split red lentils (masoor dal) or red lentils, washed and drained

1 teaspoon turmeric

½ small eggplant (aubergine), diced

¼ small cauliflower, divided into small florets

12 green beans, trimmed and diced

1 large tomato, chopped

½–1 teaspoon salt, or to taste

chopped coriander (cilantro) leaves to garnish

Sambar Paste

2 tablespoons split yellow peas

¼ teaspoon ground fenugreek

1 teaspoon chilli powder

1 teaspoon ground cumin

2 tablespoons ground coriander

3 tablespoons desiccated (grated dried) coconut

1 tablespoon tamarind pulp (page 14)

Tempering

30 g (1 oz) ghee (page 13) or salted butter

½ teaspoon black mustard seeds

1 teaspoon cumin seeds

¼ teaspoon fenugreek seeds

2 whole dried red chillies

20 curry leaves

1 small onion, chopped

Put the lentils, turmeric and 750 ml (25½ fl oz/3 cups) water in a large saucepan over a medium heat. Bring to a boil and cook uncovered for about 30 minutes, or until the lentils are soft.

Meanwhile, to make the sambar paste, grind the split yellow peas using a mortar and pestle or an electric spice grinder. Transfer to a small bowl and mix together with the fenugreek, chilli powder, cumin, coriander, coconut and tamarind pulp to form a paste.

When the lentils are cooked, stir in the sambar paste, eggplant, cauliflower, green beans and tomato and cook over a medium heat for 15 minutes. Add the salt to taste.

About 5 minutes before the sambar is ready, make the tempering. Heat the ghee or butter in a small frying pan over a high heat. Add the mustard, cumin and fenugreek seeds, dried chillies and curry leaves, and heat until they begin to crackle. Immediately add the onion and sauté, stirring occasionally, for about 5 minutes, or until golden brown.

Pour the tempering over the sambar, garnish with the chopped coriander and serve.

Poppy Seed Potatoes

Serves 4

A distinctive potato dish from Bengal, which is easy but special. Ground white poppy seeds are usually used in rich kormas and curries for a nutty, creamy texture and taste. In this radically different combination, the humble potato is teamed with white poppy seeds, one of the world's most luxurious spices. Serve this dish as part of an Indian meal.

1 tablespoon mustard oil or
    vegetable or canola oil
    (see Note)

1 teaspoon nigella (kalonji)

1 teaspoon chopped
    green chilli

1 tablespoon white poppy
    seeds, finely ground

4 large potatoes, peeled
    and diced

½ teaspoon turmeric

½–1 teaspoon salt, or to taste

Heat the oil in a small saucepan over a high heat. If you are using mustard oil, wait until it is smoking. Reduce the heat to very low and add the nigella and green chilli, then immediately stir in the poppy seeds.

Stir in the potato, turmeric, salt and 125 ml (4 fl oz/½ cup) water. Cover and cook over a very low heat for about 20 minutes, or until the potato is soft and the water is absorbed. Serve hot.

Note: You can substitute vegetable or canola oil for the mustard oil, but the dish will have a different and less distinctive and authentic flavour than if you use mustard oil.

Potatoes with Cumin Seeds

Serves 4

When designing the perfect menu, we often need a vegetable accompaniment that will not take away from the main event. This is just such a recipe. Delicious in its own right, it also complements many other flavours, so you can either serve it simply with Pooris (page 204) or Parathas (page 206), or make it part of an Indian meal.

15 g (½ oz) ghee (page 13) or
    1 tablespoon vegetable or
    canola oil

1 whole dried red chilli

1 teaspoon cumin seeds

4 large potatoes, peeled and
    diced

1 teaspoon turmeric

½–1 teaspoon salt, or to taste

Heat the ghee or oil in a small wok or frying pan with a tight-fitting lid over a medium heat. Add the chilli and cumin seeds and heat until they begin to crackle. Immediately add the potato, turmeric, salt and 60 ml (2 fl oz/¼ cup) water and stir to mix through.

Reduce the heat to low, cover the wok or pan tightly and cook for about 20 minutes, or until the potato is soft. Serve immediately.

Spinach Kadhi

Serves 4

Kadhi is a great substitute for dal and is often eaten with steamed rice. The most popular version of kadhi is made with besan (chickpea flour) dumplings. This recipe uses spinach, and is a delicious speedy alternative. Use white radish (daikon) or mustard greens instead, if you prefer vegetables with a slightly bitter flavour.

110 g (4 oz/1 cup) besan (chickpea flour)

125 g (4½ oz/½ cup) plain yoghurt

1 teaspoon turmeric

30 g (1 oz) ghee (page 13) or 1½ tablespoons mustard oil

1 small onion, sliced

1 teaspoon cumin seeds

2 dried whole red chillies

pinch of asafoetida

½–1 teaspoon salt, to taste

50 g (1¾ oz) English spinach, washed, drained and finely chopped

1 tablespoon chopped mint leaves

In a large bowl mix together the besan, yoghurt, turmeric and 500 ml (17 fl oz/2 cups) water to make a smooth paste.

Heat the ghee or oil in a medium saucepan over a medium heat. Sauté the onion, stirring occasionally for about 5 minutes, or until golden brown. Add the cumin seeds, chillies and asafoetida, and stir to mix well. Add the paste, salt and another 500 ml (17 fl oz/2 cups) water to obtain a thin sauce-like consistency.

Cook, stirring continuously, for about 30 minutes, or until the kadhi thickens. The final consistency should be like a thick soup.

Add the spinach and mint and briefly bring to the boil. Remove from the heat and serve immediately.

Mango and Pineapple Salad

Serves 4

Salads are eaten with the meal all over India, especially in the north, south and west. They provide a fresh, crisp, sweet, sour or tangy taste as well as textural excitement, which contrast well with, and helps to cut through, the richness of Indian food. Salads may be cooked or raw, using vegetables, fruits, sprouted lentils or even puffed or flattened rice. Most people outside of India do not appreciate the wide variety of salad dishes eaten routinely in Indian homes. Serve this tangy, sweet, spicy salad as an accompaniment to a meal, or as an appetiser.

2 dried whole red chillies

¼ teaspoon black mustard seeds

60 ml (2 fl oz/¼ cup) unsweetened pineapple juice

1 mango, peeled and stone removed, diced

1 small pineapple, peeled and central core removed, diced

125 g (4½ oz) fresh coconut flesh, diced

½ teaspoon finely chopped fresh ginger

juice of 1 lime

80 g (2¾ oz/½ cup) unsalted roasted peanuts (optional)

Tempering

1 tablespoon vegetable or canola oil

1 teaspoon black mustard seeds

10 curry leaves

Heat the chillies in a heavy-based frying pan over a medium heat for 1 minute. Allow to cool, then grind finely with the mustard seeds using a mortar and pestle or an electric spice grinder.

Transfer to a large bowl and gradually whisk in the pineapple juice. (Whisk vigorously so the juice forms an emulsion with the spices, rather than being a liquid with bits of spice floating in it.) Add the mango, pineapple, coconut and ginger, pour over the lime juice and toss to combine well.

To make the tempering, heat the oil in a small frying pan over a medium heat. Add the mustard seeds and curry leaves and heat until they begin to crackle.

Scatter the peanuts, if using, over the salad, then immediately pour the tempering over and serve.

Onion Salad

Serves 4

Most Indians are partial to the crunch of raw red (Spanish) onions in a salad. It adds taste and texture when eaten with curries, kababs or snacks. Other members of the allium family including shallots, red onions or even leeks and spring onions (scallions) can be used for variations in texture and flavour. The raw taste of the onion is mitigated by combining it with the acidity of different vinegars or lemon or lime juice.

2 large red (Spanish) onions, sliced

juice of 1 lime

pinch of chaat masala (page 11)

1 tablespoon finely chopped mint leaves

1 tablespoon finely chopped coriander (cilantro) leaves

1 tablespoon finely chopped red or green chilli

½–1 teaspoon salt, or to taste

Toss together the onion, lime juice, chaat masala, mint, coriander, chilli and salt in a serving bowl.

Leave at room temperature for 20 minutes to allow the flavours to combine a little, then serve.

ACCOMPANIMENTS

The diversity of flavours, textures and temperatures in Indian cuisine can, in part, be attributed to the vast array of accompaniments that come in the form of fresh sauces, dips, chutneys, breads and raitas that are served alongside curries and side dishes. No Indian meal is complete without them.

The term 'chutney' is used very loosely in India and refers not just to store-bought preserved chutneys, but also homemade fresh fruit and vegetable chutneys such as Plum Chutney (page 190) and Eggplant Chutney (page 193), or dipping sauces made with fresh herbs such as Green Chutney (page 188) and yoghurts with spice and herb infusions.

To accompany these sauces the importance of bread cannot be underestimated in an Indian meal, especially in the north, where rice is eaten less frequently. Plain (all-purpose) flour, wholemeal (whole-wheat) flour, atta flour or even besan (chickpea flour) is used to make leavened or unleavened, baked, pan-cooked or fried breads, which may be served to accompany vegetables, lentils or meat, or even just rolled with butter and jam for a simple tea-time treat.

The accompaniments in this chapter are quick and easy to prepare. Make sure you use the freshest seasonal ingredients available to allow the simple flavours to shine through. Mix and match breads with raitas, or try making your own chutneys in addition to the recipes in this chapter by experimenting with left-over fruits and vegetables in your kitchen. Once you master the technique of making them, you will never return to store-bought chutneys.

Tamarind and Ginger Chutney

Makes 250 ml (8½ fl oz/1 cup)

This piquant, sweet-and-sour fresh chutney comes from North India. It is an important part of chaat, the famous street food that brings together crisp, savoury discs made of semolina or plain (all-purpose) flour with roasted vegetables, puffed rice and fried besan (chickpea flour) vermicelli. As well as being an integral part of chaat, this chutney goes well with salads, potato patties, boiled chickpeas, Pakoras (page 26) and Vegetable Samosas (page 28).

100 g (3½ oz) dried tamarind

1 tablespoon chopped fresh ginger

1 teaspoon chilli powder

1 teaspoon chaat masala (page 11)

100 g (3½ oz) sugar

banana slices to garnish

Put the dried tamarind, ginger, chilli powder, chaat masala, sugar and 500 ml (17 fl oz/2 cups) water in a small saucepan. Stir until the sugar has dissolved, then bring to a boil over a high heat. Reduce the heat to low and simmer for 30 minutes.

Strain the mixture through a mesh strainer to give a homogenous thick liquid, without any seeds, flesh or fibres from the tamarind or ginger. Chill the chutney in the refrigerator for at least 20 minutes, or until ready to serve. Garnish with banana slices before serving.

Mint Chutney

Makes 250 ml (8½ fl oz/1 cup)

Dark green mint chutney is a refreshing, bold dipping sauce, which accompanies fried starters and tandoori kababs, or is used in chaat (see opposite). Indian cooking depends on many extras, such as this one, to provide a clean, contrasting flavour. In India the term 'chutney' describes a wide range of accompaniments. It can include long-lasting chutneys in jars, other chutneys that are fresh and will keep for two to three months, and still others that are really dipping or accompanying sauces, such as this one. This chutney will keep in the refrigerator for up to four days.

50 g (1¾ oz) mint leaves
juice of 1 lemon or lime
1 clove garlic
1 tablespoon sugar
1 teaspoon salt
2 green chillies

Process the mint, lemon or lime juice, garlic, sugar, salt and chillies with 125 ml (4 fl oz/½ cup) water in a food processor to form a smooth paste.

Chill the chutney in the refrigerator for 20 minutes, until the flavours have infused, or until ready to serve.

Green Chutney

Makes 375 ml (13 fl oz/1½ cups)

Found in almost every Indian restaurant and takeaway, green chutney is the perfect accompaniment for fried foods such as Vegetable Samosas (page 28) or Pakoras (page 26), or tandoori foods. Follow this recipe and you will find yourself taken to a whole new flavour level altogether. Serve it chilled with snacks and starters. It will keep in the refrigerator for up to four days.

25 g (1 oz) chopped mint leaves

25 g (1 oz) chopped coriander (cilantro) leaves

2 green chillies, chopped

1 garlic clove, chopped

1 small onion, chopped

1 tablespoon sugar

1 teaspoon salt

125 g (4½ oz/½ cup) plain yoghurt

Put the mint, coriander, chilli, garlic, onion, sugar, salt and yoghurt in a food processor, and blend together to form a completely smooth paste, with no flecks of chopped herbs visible.

Chill the chutney in the refrigerator for 30 minutes, until the flavours have infused, or until ready to serve.

Note: It is important to chop up all the ingredients before blending them. This is so you can produce the smoothest paste possible using the least amount of liquid. This will not work efficiently if large bunches of herbs are put in the food processor.

Coconut Chutney

Makes 250 ml (8½ fl oz/1 cup)

Fresh coconut chutney, just tempered with herbs and spices, has an important place in South Indian cooking. The fresh flavour of coconut gives a soothing feel to snacks and starters. The chutney will keep in the refrigerator for up to two days.

45 g (1½ oz/½ cup) desiccated (grated dried) coconut or 60 g (2 oz) freshly grated coconut

1 small green chilli

1 teaspoon chopped fresh ginger

½–1 teaspoon salt, or to taste

1 tablespoon vegetable or canola oil

12 curry leaves

2 whole dried red chillies

½ teaspoon black mustard seeds

Process the coconut, green chilli, ginger and salt in a food processor, adding up to 250 ml (8½ fl oz/1 cup) warm water a little at a time until the mixture forms a finely ground paste. Transfer to a bowl.

Heat the oil in a small frying pan over a medium heat. Add the curry leaves, dried chillies and mustard seeds, and heat until they begin to crackle. Immediately pour over the coconut mixture and stir through to combine.

Serve at room temperature.

Plum Chutney

Makes 1 litre (34 fl oz/4 cups)

At the Spice Kitchen we make all our own fruit chutneys and we use any seasonal fruit that is available. Some of our chutneys are bottled to sell, but most are served as accompaniments at the restaurant. I love this plum chutney with a simple meat curry such as Lamb Kata Masala (page 142). Plum chutney and other fruit chutneys will generally keep in the refrigerator for up to three weeks. They are eaten in larger quantities than their sharper, hotter cousins, and add more liquid to the meal.

2 tablespoons vegetable or canola oil

2.5 cm (1 in) cinnamon stick

4 cloves

1 small onion, diced

500 g (1 lb 2 oz) plums, halved and stoned

220 g (8 oz/1 cup) sugar

1 teaspoon chilli powder

1 tablespoon ginger paste (page 12)

1 tablespoon garlic paste (page 12)

1½ tablespoons white vinegar

Heat the oil in a large saucepan over a medium heat. Sauté the cinnamon, cloves and onion, stirring occasionally, for about 2 minutes, or until the onion is translucent.

Add the plums, sugar, chilli powder, ginger and garlic pastes and vinegar, and stir until the sugar has dissolved. Cook over a medium heat for about 45 minutes, or until the plums are soft and almost all of the liquid has evaporated.

Leave the chutney to cool before serving – there is no need to remove the whole spices.

Dahi Chutney

Makes 500 ml (17 fl oz/2 cups)

Dahi chutney is a chopped coriander and mint chutney with green chillies and yoghurt. It is quite spicy and is traditionally served with Hyderabadi biryani. It is thicker and chunkier than Green Chutney (page 188), more like a raita in texture. It will keep in the refrigerator for up to two days.

250 g (9 oz/1 cup) plain yoghurt

1 onion, chopped

2 green chillies, chopped

small handful mint leaves, chopped

small handful coriander (cilantro) leaves, chopped

½–1 teaspoon salt, or to taste

Mix together the yoghurt, onion, chilli, mint, coriander and salt in a small bowl.

Chill the chutney in the refrigerator for 15 minutes, until the flavours have infused, or until ready to serve.

Sesame Chutney

Makes 185 ml (6½ fl oz/¾ cup)

Although not as popular as the ubiquitous Green Chutney (page 188), this is nevertheless a deliciously herby, nutty complement to kababs and roasted meat dishes. It can also be used as a delicious dip for vegetables – an Indian tahini with spice. It will keep in the refrigerator for up to two days.

1 tablespoon sesame seeds, roasted and coarsely ground (page 10)

3 green chillies

large handful mint leaves

1 small onion, chopped

1 tablespoon chopped garlic

2 tablespoons tamarind pulp (page 14)

½–1 teaspoon salt, or to taste

Put the sesame seeds, chillies, mint, onion, garlic and tamarind in a food processor and process to make a smooth paste. Transfer to a bowl, add the salt and mix together well.

Serve at room temperature or chill in the refrigerator until ready to serve.

Eggplant Chutney

Makes 1 litre (34 fl oz/4 cups)

Indian homes abound with chutneys and pickles that add another dimension to everyday eating. Fresh chutneys can be made with any vegetables in season, and in fact, they are a good way of using up excess garden produce. You could use carrots, tomatoes, turnips, cauliflower or pumpkin (winter squash) to make chutneys and relishes. Vegetable chutneys will generally keep in the refrigerator for about two months. This eggplant chutney, however, must be served fresh, and will only keep in the refrigerator for one day. Serve it as a dip or to accompany an Indian meal.

2 eggplants (aubergines)

45 g (1½ oz/½ cup) desiccated (grated dried) coconut or 60 g (2 oz) freshly grated coconut

2 whole dried red chillies, roasted (page 10)

¼ teaspoon ginger paste (page 12)

¼ teaspoon garlic paste (page 12)

2 teaspoons tamarind pulp (page 14)

40 g (1½ oz/¼ cup) unsalted roasted peanuts

2 tablespoons palm syrup or dark brown sugar or molasses

½–1 teaspoon salt, or to taste

Roast the eggplant whole in a heavy-based frying pan or chargrill pan over a medium heat, or under the grill (broiler), for about 20 minutes, or until soft and the skin is charred. Turn only once or twice during cooking. Allow to cool, then cut in half. Scoop out the flesh with a spoon, chop roughly and reserve. Discard the skin.

Put the eggplant flesh, coconut, chillies, ginger and garlic pastes, tamarind, peanuts, palm syrup or dark brown sugar or molasses and salt in a food processor, and process to form a thick, chunky consistency or, more traditionally, a smooth paste. Serve at room temperature.

Tomato Chutney

Makes 500 ml (17 fl oz/2 cups)

A traditional menu in Bengal always starts with something bitter, using vegetables, and ends with something sweet. This is true whether you are eating an everyday lunch or dinner, or celebrating an event, such as a wedding. Tomato chutney is a must at the end of the Bengali meal and it is deliciously fresh. It will keep in the refrigerator for up to one week.

1 tablespoon mustard oil or vegetable or canola oil

1 teaspoon panch phoron (page 12)

2 whole dried red chillies

1 tablespoon ginger paste (page 12)

4 large tomatoes, roughly chopped

110 g (4 oz/½ cup) sugar

½–1 teaspoon salt, or to taste

Heat the oil in a large saucepan over a medium heat. If you are using mustard oil, wait until it is smoking. Heat the panch phoron and chillies until they begin to crackle. Immediately stir in the ginger paste and sauté for 2 minutes.

Stir in the tomato, sugar and salt, and cook, stirring occasionally, for 10 minutes, or until the tomato is soft. Remove from the heat and leave to cool.

Serve at room temperature.

Lime Juice Chutney

Makes 250 ml (8½ fl oz/1 cup)

Pickles and chutneys are an integral part of a well-balanced Indian meal. Contrasting tastes, textures and temperatures all play their part in making your plate tantalisingly appealing to your taste buds. With most chutneys, you start out with whole ingredients, such as herbs, vegetables or fruit, which are chopped and then processed to a paste. This recipe is an exception because it starts with a juice – lime juice. The resulting syrupy consistency is fantastic for serving as a dipping sauce for Masala Pappadums (page 22) or drizzled over fried fish or prawns (shrimp). Lime juice chutney will keep in the refrigerator for at least one month.

1 tablespoon vegetable or canola oil

½ teaspoon black mustard seeds

250 ml (8½ fl oz/1 cup) lime juice

220 g (8 oz/1 cup) sugar

1 teaspoon asafoetida

1 teaspoon chilli powder

½ teaspoon turmeric

½–1 teaspoon salt, or to taste

Heat the oil in a large saucepan over a medium heat. Add the mustard seeds and heat until they begin to crackle. Immediately add the lime juice, sugar, asafoetida, chilli powder, turmeric and salt, and stir until the sugar has dissolved.

Reduce the heat to low and cook uncovered for about 30 minutes, or until the liquid has thickened to a syrup.

Cool, then chill in the refrigerator for at least 20 minutes, or until ready to serve.

Cucumber Raita

Makes 500 ml (17 fl oz/2 cups)

Not many meals in India would be complete without yoghurt in some form. This might be plain yoghurt, a raita or a sweetened yoghurt. Most Indian families set their own yoghurt at home, but a good-quality store-bought organic yoghurt is a perfectly acceptable alternative. The most popular of all raitas, cucumber raita, goes especially well with chicken curries. Make sure you remove the seeds from the cucumber or use a seedless variety. And any left-over raita will keep in the refrigerator for up to three days.

250 g (9 oz/1 cup) plain yoghurt

½ cucumber, peeled if desired and seeds removed, grated (see Note)

1 tablespoon finely chopped onion

½–1 teaspoon salt, or to taste

1 teaspoon yellow mustard seeds, roasted and ground (page 10)

2 teaspoons cumin seeds, roasted and ground (page 10)

¼ teaspoon red chilli powder

Put the yoghurt, cucumber, onion, salt and all but a pinch each of the yellow mustard, cumin and chilli powder in a small bowl. Mix together, then chill in the refrigerator for at least 20 minutes, or until ready to serve.

Transfer the raita to a serving bowl, sprinkle over the remaining pinch of yellow mustard, cumin and chilli powder, and serve.

Note: Raitas are meant to be of a pouring consistency – not too thick. But if you prefer a more solid texture and consistency, squeeze the grated cucumber between your palms to remove all the liquid from it before mixing with the yoghurt.

Variation: To make a Spinach Raita, heat 2 teaspoons of canola oil in a small frying pan and gently fry 50 g (1¾ oz) baby spinach with ½ teaspoon garlic paste (page 12) and 1 whole red chilli until the spinach has wilted. Leave to cool, then transfer to a small bowl and add the yoghurt, stirring gently to combine. Season to taste, and chill for 20 minutes or until ready to serve.

Boondi Raita

Makes 500 ml (17 fl oz/2 cups)

Raitas are yoghurt salads eaten with the main meal to provide a fresh balance for the palate. Plain yoghurt may be combined with raw salad vegetables, steamed or roasted vegetables such as corn or eggplant (aubergine), fruit and sometimes even seafood or bone marrow. Boondi raita comes from North India. It is a mix of boondis – which are tiny balls, or droplets, of besan (chickpea flour), deep-fried – plain yoghurt and spices. Even though some people think of raitas as being 'cooling' and thus unspiced, a good raita will always have one or two spices to enhance its main ingredients.

Boondis

110 g (4 oz/1 cup) besan (chickpea flour)

pinch of salt

vegetable or canola oil for deep-frying

Raita

250 g (9 oz/1 cup) plain yoghurt

½–1 teaspoon salt, or to taste

½ teaspoon yellow mustard seeds, roasted and ground (page 10)

1 teaspoon cumin seeds, roasted and ground (page 10)

¼ teaspoon red chilli powder

To make the boondis, whisk together the besan, salt and 125 ml (4 fl oz/½ cup) water in a medium bowl to make a stiff batter.

Heat the oil in a wok or deep-fryer to 200°C (400°F) (see page 15). Using a frying spoon with round holes (see Note), get a spoonful of batter, hold it over the wok or deep-fryer (about 10 cm/4 in from the hot oil to avoid splashing) and press down on the batter with a ladle or other object with a flat unbroken surface to force the batter through the holes in the frying spoon. Little balls of batter will drop into the hot oil and solidify immediately. Deep-fry until golden brown, turning frequently with a clean slotted spoon, for about 1 minute. Remove from the oil and drain on kitchen towels. Leave to cool while deep-frying the remaining boondi batter.

Soak the boondis in a bowl of warm water for 10 minutes, until they swell to about double their size. Gently squeeze the boondis to remove excess water, being careful not to break them.

To make the raita, put the yoghurt, boondis, salt and all but a pinch each of the yellow mustard, cumin and chilli powder in a small bowl. Mix together, then chill in the refrigerator for at least 15 minutes, or until ready to serve.

Transfer the raita to a serving bowl, sprinkle over the remaining pinch of yellow mustard, cumin and chilli powder, and serve.

Note: *There are boondi spoons specially designed to make this dish, but any frying spoon with round holes will work. Look for a slotted spoon with round holes in Indian and Asian grocery stores.*

199

Naan

Makes 4–6

Naan is a leavened bread, made with plain (all-purpose) wheat flour and cooked on the walls of the tandoor oven. Real naan needs a tandoor, where the temperatures can reach up to 400°C (750°F), and it is impossible to replicate this at home. But this recipe is the next best thing if you really want to make fresh naan. It is perfect with any barbecued or tandoori food, kababs, kormas and rich curries.

225 g (8 oz/1½ cups) plain (all-purpose) flour

75 g (2¾ oz/½ cup) self-raising flour

pinch of salt

1 teaspoon sugar

250 ml (8½ fl oz/1 cup) milk

1 tablespoon plain yoghurt

1 egg

1 tablespoon vegetable or canola oil

1 tablespoon nigella (kalonji)

melted butter for glazing

Mix together the plain and self-raising flours, salt and sugar in a large bowl, then make a well in the centre. Add the milk, yoghurt, egg and oil and work through the dry ingredients to combine, adding a little more milk if necessary to form a soft dough. Turn out onto a lightly floured work surface and knead for 10 minutes, or until the dough feels smooth and elastic. Place the dough in a clean bowl, cover with a damp cloth and set aside in a warm place to rise for 8 hours. The dough should rise by about half its size, and will have a yeasty smell and feel more pliable.

Divide the dough into 4–6 balls about 5 cm (2 in) in diameter, cover with a damp cloth and rest for 20 minutes.

Put a heavy baking tray under the grill (broiler) and, being sure to leave the grill door open, preheat the grill to high for at least 20 minutes. Alternatively, put a heavy baking tray on the top shelf or rack of the oven, close the door and preheat the oven to 200°C (400°F).

Press out each dough ball with your fingers to shape it into a triangle about 5 mm (¼ in) thick. Sprinkle with a little water, and then sprinkle over the nigella (the water helps the nigella to stick to the dough). Place on the heavy baking tray and grill under the grill or bake on the top shelf of the oven for about 2 minutes, or until brown flecks appear on the surface, then turn over and grill or bake on the top shelf for a further 40 seconds.

Brush with a little melted butter and serve immediately.

Variations: **To make garlic naan, brush a triangle of dough with ½ teaspoon garlic paste (page 12) before cooking.**

To make cheese naan, stuff the centre of each dough ball with 2 tablespoons grated mature cheddar cheese before resting for 20 minutes, then continue as for the recipe above.

Chapattis

Makes 4–6

This favourite home-style flat bread is made from unleavened atta flour, a finely ground wholemeal (whole-wheat) flour made from durum wheat. Traditionally, chapattis are served fresh from the kitchen one at a time and are usually pounced upon as soon as they hit the table. And if you can't eat them all straight away, you can freeze them, then thaw as needed and reheat in the microwave.

150 g (5½ oz/1 cup) atta flour
ghee (page 13) to serve
   (optional)

Put the flour in a large bowl and make a well in the centre. Gradually pour in 125 ml (4 fl oz/½ cup) water while working in the flour, adding a little more water if necessary to form a soft dough. Turn out onto a lightly floured work surface and knead for 15 minutes, or until the dough is pliable and not sticky. Place the dough in a clean bowl, cover with a damp cloth and rest for 30 minutes.

Divide the dough into 4–6 balls, each about the size of a golf ball. On a lightly floured work surface, roll out each piece of dough until it is thin like a tortilla, and about 18 cm (7 in) in diameter.

Heat a heavy-based frying pan over a medium heat. Dry-cook each chapatti for about 1 minute, then turn over and cook the other side for a further 40 seconds, carefully pressing down around the edges of the chapatti with a clean tea towel (dish towel) until it puffs up in the centre.

Spread with a little ghee, if desired, and serve immediately.

Pooris

Makes 10

Pooris are a quintessential street food, fried in open kitchens in city cafés, or on food carts in train and bus stations. They are a traditional part of the thali meal – an array of five or six curries, both meat and vegetarian, presented in little bowls or on a metal plate along with rice, pickles and chutneys. Pooris are usually served with a simple potato or pumpkin curry, sometimes with sweet dishes such as a rice pudding, or most simply of all, just sprinkled with sugar. They can be covered with plastic wrap and kept at room temperature for six to eight hours. If you are keeping them for longer, put them in the refrigerator, where they will last for up to two days.

150 g (5½ oz/1 cup) atta flour

pinch of salt

30 g (1 oz) ghee (page 13) or 2 tablespoons vegetable or canola oil

vegetable or canola oil for deep-frying

Put the flour, salt and ghee or oil in a large bowl. Gradually pour in 125 ml (4 fl oz/½ cup) water while working the ingredients together, adding a little more water if necessary to make a stiff but not sticky dough, which is not very pliable but holds together well. Turn out onto a lightly floured work surface and knead for 5 minutes, or until the dough feels smooth and holds together as one piece without sticking. Place the dough in a clean bowl, cover with a damp cloth and rest for 20 minutes.

Divide the dough into 10 balls, each about the size of a large marble. On a lightly oiled work surface, roll out each piece of dough with a rolling pin to form a small circle about 5 cm (2 in) in diameter and 1 cm (½ in) thick.

Heat the oil in a wok or deep-fryer to 200°C (400°F) (see page 15).

Deep-fry each poori for about 40 seconds, or until golden brown and puffed up, turning once with a slotted spoon and using the spoon to lightly press down on the poori as it puffs up. Remove from the oil and drain on kitchen towels. Serve hot.

Missie Roti

Makes 6–8

In North India, many kinds of flour are used to make breads. This is a part of India where hardly any rice is eaten at all. Atta (from durum wheat), corn, besan (chickpea flour), millet, rye, ragi (from finger millet) and other flours all produce hearty, peasant-style breads. Missie roti is a rustic, home-style spicy flat bread, low in carbohydrates, that highlights the nutty flavour of besan. Serve with plain yoghurt for a quick snack, breakfast or brunch dish.

150 g (5½ oz/1 cup) atta flour or plain (all-purpose) flour (see Note)

55 g (2 oz/½ cup) besan (chickpea flour)

½ teaspoon chilli flakes

pinch of asafoetida

½–1 teaspoon salt, or to taste

1 tablespoon dried fenugreek leaves

ghee (page 13) or plain yoghurt to serve

Put the atta or plain flour, besan, chilli, asafoetida and salt in a large bowl. Crush the fenugreek leaves between your hands and add to the bowl, then mix together. Gradually pour in 190 ml (6½ fl oz/¾ cup) water while working the ingredients together, adding a little more water if necessary to make a flexible dough that does not stick to the sides of the bowl. Turn out onto a lightly floured work surface and knead for 10 minutes, or until pliable but not sticky. Place the dough in a clean bowl, cover with a damp cloth and rest for 30 minutes.

Divide the dough into 6–8 balls, each about the size of a golf ball. On a lightly floured work surface, roll out each piece of dough until it is thin like a tortilla and about 6–8 cm (2½ in–3¼ in) in diameter. (This dough is not elastic, and so the roti may be irregular or slightly cracked, which suits this rustic, strongly flavoured bread.)

Heat a heavy-based frying pan over a medium heat. Dry-cook each roti for about 1 minute, then turn and cook the other side for a further 1 minute. The bread is done when it lightens in colour and little brown flecks appear on the surface.

Spread each roti with a little ghee before serving, or serve with yoghurt on the side.

Note: You can use plain flour instead of atta flour, but the rotis will have a slightly different taste and texture.

205

Parathas

Makes 6–8

Parathas – plain or wholemeal (whole-wheat) unleavened bread – are eaten for breakfast, lunch or dinner. They are also great for picnics and travel snacks. Spread a paratha with yoghurt or your favourite fruit jam, eat it simply with vegetables, or roll up a paratha 'wrap'. You can also use this recipe as the basis for making stuffed parathas (see Variation below).

300 g (10 oz/2 cups) atta flour

1 teaspoon salt

125 g (4½ oz/½ cup) ghee (page 13)

additional atta flour for dusting

Mix together the flour and salt in a large bowl, then make a well in the centre. Add 2 tablespoons of the ghee and gradually pour in 190 ml (6½ fl oz/¾ cup) warm water while working the ingredients together, adding more water as necessary to make a pliable dough that does not stick to the side of the bowl. Turn out onto a lightly floured work surface and knead for 5 minutes. Place the dough in a clean bowl, cover with a damp cloth and rest for 30 minutes.

Divide the dough into 6–8 balls, each about the size of a golf ball. Using a rolling pin, roll out each piece of dough on a lightly floured work surface to form a small circle about 5 cm (2 in) in diameter. Spread with a little ghee and fold in half to form a hemisphere, then spread with ghee and fold it in half again to form a triangle with a curved edge. Dust with atta flour and roll out into a triangle that is 3 mm (⅛ in) thick.

Heat a heavy-based frying pan over a medium heat. Dry-cook each paratha on one side for about 1 minute, then spread with a little of the remaining ghee, turn over and cook the other side for 1 minute. It is cooked when light brown flecks appear on the underside. Spread the upper side with a little ghee, turn over again and cook for a further 30 seconds. Serve immediately.

Variation: You can make stuffed parathas with fillings such as mashed potato, grated radish or cauliflower mixed with a little salt and chilli powder. Put 1 teaspoon of filling in the middle of a 5 cm (2 in) circle of dough, then gather up the edges of the circle around the stuffing and bring them together and seal into little balls. Roll out into a thin circular shape, dust with atta flour and follow the cooking instructions for plain parathas.

Bhaturas

Makes 4–6

A leavened deep-fried bread that uses plain (all-purpose) flour, the bhatura is cooked in little cafés all over Delhi and Punjab. It is a quintessential street food, sold from road carts. University students and office workers queue up for hours for bhatura and chickpeas. Everyone has a favourite vendor and the merits of each are hotly debated. Serve them with Chickpea Masala (page 55).

300 g (10½ oz/2 cups) plain (all-purpose) flour

75 g (2¾ oz/½ cup) self-raising flour

1 teaspoon salt

¼ teaspoon sugar

60 g (2 oz/¼ cup) plain yoghurt

30 g (1 oz) ghee (page 13) or vegetable or canola oil

vegetable or canola oil for deep-frying

Mix together the plain and self-raising flours, salt and sugar, then make a well in the centre. Add the yoghurt, ghee or oil, and 625 ml (21 fl oz/2½ cups) warm water and work through the dry ingredients to combine, adding a little more water if necessary. Knead for 8 minutes to form a sticky dough. Cover with a damp cloth, then set aside in a warm place to rise for at least 2 hours, or until it is pliable and stretchy.

Turn out onto a lightly floured work surface and knead the dough again for 5 minutes. Divide it into 4–6 balls about 3 cm (1¼ in) in diameter, cover with a damp cloth and rest for 10–15 minutes.

Oil the palms of your hands, then press and spread out each ball of dough with your fingers to form a circle about 10 cm (4 in) in diameter and 5 mm (¼ in) thick. Alternatively, roll out each piece of dough with a rolling pin on a lightly floured work surface.

Heat the oil in a wok or deep-fryer to 200°C (400°F) (see page 15). (It is crucial that these breads are deep-fried in very hot oil.)

Carefully put a round of dough in the very hot oil. Lightly press a slotted spoon down on the dough for about 5 seconds and then lift it off. (Pressing down for a few seconds at the start of the deep-frying compresses the steam inside the round of dough, and when the weight of the spoon is lifted off, the released steam causes the bhatura to gradually puff up during the cooking time.) Deep-fry each bhatura for about 2 minutes, or until golden brown and puffed up, turning once with the slotted spoon. Remove from the oil and drain on kitchen towels. Serve hot.

Fried Onions

Makes 100 g (3½ oz)

*Crisp, golden brown fried onions are used in many
Indian recipes. They can be mixed with other ingredients
at the end of the cooking process to provide a crunch,
or added to a marinade to imbue all the ingredients
with their characteristic sweetness. They can also be
scattered simply over steamed rice or used right at the
end, as a garnish. They can be stored in an airtight
container at room temperature or in the refrigerator
for two to three days.*

2 large brown onions, thinly
    sliced
pinch of salt
100 g (3½ oz) ghee (page 13) or
    100 ml (3½ fl oz) vegetable or
    canola oil (see Note)

Put the onion in a colander, sprinkle over the salt and
leave for 20 minutes. Squeeze all the liquid out of the
onion by pressing and squeezing it between the palms
of your hands.

Heat the ghee or oil in a medium saucepan over a
medium heat. Sauté the onions in four separate batches,
stirring frequently, for 2 minutes or until golden brown
and crisp. Remove from the heat and use as desired.

*Note: You can use vegetable or canola oil instead of ghee for frying
the onion, but the flavour will not be as refined.*

Straw Potatoes

Makes 150 g (5½ oz)

*Crisp-fried straw potatoes can be served with an
Indian meal or they can be a component in a dish, such
as Parsee lamb curry or akuri, the Parsee version of
scrambled eggs.*

vegetable or canola oil for
    deep-frying
2 large potatoes, peeled and cut
    into matchsticks
½–1 teaspoon salt, or to taste

Heat the oil in a wok or deep-fryer to 200°C (400°F)
(see page 15).

Deep-fry the potato in small batches, stirring frequently
with a slotted spoon, for about 8 minutes, or until golden
brown and crisp. Remove from the oil with the slotted
spoon and drain on kitchen towels.

Sprinkle with the salt and serve hot or at room
temperature.

DESSERTS

Desserts are not usually considered when preparing an everyday Indian meal, as the preceding dishes are often so rich, with multiple components. Many Indians choose to finish a meal with a simple bowl of yoghurt, maybe sweetened or served with fresh fruit. I must admit there is nothing quite like the taste of a perfectly ripened mango served with yoghurt after a richly flavoured meal.

However, many Indians do have a very sweet tooth and desserts always feature on the menu at special and festive occasions. Kulfi, the popular Indian ice cream, is a favourite at the Spice Kitchen and can easily be recreated at home. There are three kulfi recipes in this chapter – Passionfruit Kulfi (page 214), Mango Kulfi (page 231) and a Christmas Kulfi (page 224) for a festive variation that can be served instead of Christmas pudding. Traditionally, kulfi is made by reducing milk over a low heat for a long time, but today evaporated and condensed milk is used to speed up the process. You can make kulfi with any fresh fruits, so experiment with whatever is in season.

In this chapter I have tried to choose recipes not only that I love, but that also show the diversity of Indian desserts – from the famous Gulab Jamun (page 226) and simple Coconut Pancakes (page 225), to the beautifully rich Vermicelli Pudding (page 220), and my own personal creation, Baked Saffron Yoghurt Pudding with Tomato Compote (page 222). Once you have mastered these recipes there really is no end to the variations that can be created from them. I hope there is something here for everyone.

Passionfruit Kulfi

Serves 6

Kulfi is an Indian almond ice cream, traditionally frozen in conical containers to resemble the Himalayan mountains. In India it is served with falooda, a cornflour (cornstarch) vermicelli, which provides a contrast in temperature, taste and texture. Kulfis are eaten on all sorts of occasions – on a casual beach outing, at the movies, or as a sweet finale to a wedding. This is a hard ice cream and should be transferred from the freezer to the refrigerator five minutes before serving, to help remove the kulfi from the mould without it melting.

315 g (11 oz/1 cup) sweetened condensed milk

500 ml (17 fl oz/2 cups) evaporated milk

375 ml (12½ fl oz/1½ cups) thick (double/heavy) cream

250 g (9 oz/1 cup) passionfruit pulp (see Note), plus extra to serve

40 g (1½ oz) ground almonds

Put the condensed and evaporated milks, cream, passionfruit and ground almonds in a large bowl and mix together until well combined.

Pour the mixture into a freezer-proof 1.5 litre (51 fl oz/6 cup) mould or terrine or into six 250 ml (8½ fl oz/1 cup) ramekins or dessert glasses. Cover with plastic wrap and freeze for at least 8 hours.

About 5 minutes before serving, transfer the kulfi to the refrigerator. When ready to serve, turn the kulfi out of the large mould or terrine, if using, onto a platter and cut into slices, or invert the individual ramekins onto plates. (If you are having difficulty getting the kulfi out, you can roll the individual ramekins between your hands to provide a little warmth and help remove the kulfi from the ramekins. However, do not run hot water over them as this will make the surface of the ice cream melt.) If you have prepared the kulfi in dessert glasses, you can serve them straight away.

Spoon the extra passionfruit pulp over the top and serve immediately.

Note: You will need 4–6 passionfruit for the kulfi, or you could use canned passionfruit pulp.

Malpuas

Serves 4

Bengal is a hotbed of literature, music, theatre, politics – and sweet delicacies. Bengali sweets made with fresh cheese, palm sugar or steamed yoghurt are famous throughout India. Most require great expertise to produce. But malpuas – fennel-scented pancakes, crisp on the outside, soft inside, and soaked in sugar syrup – can easily be made at home and will certainly have you hungry for more.

200 ml (7 fl oz) vegetable or canola oil for shallow-frying

Sugar Syrup
200 g (7 oz) sugar

Batter
150 g (5½ oz/1 cup) plain (all-purpose) flour

30 g (1 oz/¼ cup) semolina

1 tablespoon fennel seeds plus extra to garnish

370–400 ml (12½–13½ fl oz) evaporated milk

To make the sugar syrup, put the sugar and about 500 ml (17 fl oz/2 cups) water in a medium saucepan (the water should just cover the sugar) and cook, stirring, over a high heat until the sugar has dissolved and the liquid starts to bubble, for 5 minutes at the most. Reduce the heat to low and continue cooking for about 20 minutes, or until the sugar syrup is glossy but not too thick. Remove from the heat, cover with a lid and keep warm.

Meanwhile, to make the batter, sift the flour into a large bowl. Add the semolina and fennel seeds and mix together, then make a well in the centre. Pour in 300 ml (10 fl oz) of the evaporated milk and whisk together to make a lump-free batter with a pouring consistency, adding the remaining milk as necessary to form the right consistency.

When the syrup is cooked, heat the oil over a medium heat in a large frying pan (the oil should be about 5 mm/¼ in deep). Pour in a ladleful of batter and watch it spread to form a thin pancake in the oil. Cook for about 2 minutes, or until the underside is golden brown, then turn over with tongs and a frying spoon or metal spatula and cook for a further 1 minute.

Pour the sugar syrup into a large heatproof shallow bowl. Transfer the pancake to the bowl and soak in the syrup for 2–3 minutes. Repeat to use up the remaining batter and sugar syrup, and serve hot with the extra fennel seeds sprinkled over the top.

Phirnee

Serves 6

Of all the home-style desserts eaten in India, this is the easiest and the most popular. It is found all over the country, and many regions have their own variations, such as adding date palm syrup or coconut. This version of the creamy, comforting rice-flour pudding is from North India. Serve it simply as an everyday dessert or jazz it up with rose petals and edible silver leaf for a very special occasion.

30 g (1 oz) rice flour

300 ml (10 fl oz) milk

100 g (3½ oz) sugar

¼ teaspoon saffron threads

1 teaspoon green cardamom pods, crushed

almonds, unsalted roasted cashew nuts or shelled pistachio nuts, crushed or finely chopped, to garnish

Mix together the rice flour and 100 ml (3½ fl oz) of the milk in a small bowl to make a thin paste.

Put the remaining milk in a medium heavy-based saucepan over a medium heat and bring to a boil. Immediately reduce the heat to low, stir in the rice flour paste and cook, stirring continuously, for about 15 minutes or until the mixture thickens. Add the sugar, saffron and cardamom and cook, stirring, for about 8 minutes, or until the sugar has dissolved.

Pour into six dessert bowls and sprinkle with the almonds, cashew nuts or pistachio nuts. Cool to room temperature or chill in the refrigerator for about 2 hours, then serve.

Mango Rice Pudding with Cardamom and Pistachio Nuts

Serves 4

A popular home-style dessert, rice pudding can be found in many forms throughout India, using coconut milk or milk, palm syrup or rice flour. This summer version with its delectable mango flavour is a show stopper. For something very different, instead of ripe mango pulp, try using green mango pulp, which must be cooked with sugar beforehand.

110 g (4 oz/½ cup) short-grain rice

2 litres (68 fl oz/8 cups) milk

2 mangoes

3 green cardamom pods, crushed

220 g (8 oz/1 cup) sugar

mango pieces to garnish

2 tablespoons crushed shelled pistachio nuts to garnish

Mix together the rice and milk in the upper saucepan of a large double boiler that is gently simmering over a low heat. (Make sure the upper saucepan does not touch the simmering water below.) Cover the upper saucepan with a tight-fitting lid and cook the rice and milk, stirring occasionally, for at least 1½ hours, or until it is very soft and creamy. During the cooking time, check the double boiler occasionally and add more milk if necessary to make sure it does not boil dry.

Meanwhile, peel the mangoes and, using a sharp knife, remove all the mango flesh from around the stone. Process the mango flesh in a food processor until it forms a smooth pulp. Set aside.

When the rice is cooked and soft and creamy, stir in the cardamom and sugar and cook over a low heat, stirring, for about 5 minutes, or until the sugar has dissolved. Remove the rice pudding from the heat and leave to cool to room temperature, then chill in the refrigerator for 20 minutes.

Stir the reserved mango pulp through the rice pudding. Divide between four dessert glasses, garnish with the mango pieces and pistachio nuts and serve.

Variation: If you want to make a very different-flavoured version with green mango, you will need 250 g (9 oz) green mango (you can buy these from Indian or Asian grocery stores during spring and early summer). Steam the whole mango in a steamer basket over a saucepan of simmering water for 30 minutes, or until soft. Allow to cool, then, using a very sharp knife, peel the skin, and slice away all the flesh from the stone. Put the flesh and 100 g (3½ oz) sugar in a food processor and blend to make a pulp. Stir the pulp through the chilled rice pudding, garnish with pistachio nuts and serve.

Vermicelli Pudding

Serves 4–6

As children, my cousins and I often spent summer holidays with my grandparents at their home in Dehradun, a sprawling country town in the Himalayan foothills. The house was surrounded by lychee, mango, plum and peach orchards, with trees to climb, and uninterrupted lazy days of book reading, but most of all, fabulous food prepared by their hugely talented cook, Moti Singh. This dish was a particular highlight – a decadent breakfast cereal or a delicious, comforting dessert. You can buy the roasted vermicelli for this dish from Indian grocery stores.

400 ml (13½ fl oz) milk

125 ml (4 fl oz/½ cup) pouring (single/light) cream

55 g (2 oz/¼ cup) sugar

3 saffron threads

4 green cardamom pods, coarsely ground

2 tablespoons sultanas (golden raisins)

100 g (3½ oz) roasted vermicelli

chopped shelled pistachio nuts to garnish

Heat the milk in a heavy-based saucepan over a low heat. When it is hot, stir in the cream, sugar, saffron, cardamom and sultanas and simmer for about 30 minutes.

Carefully slide in the vermicelli and cook over a low heat, stirring continuously, for about 15 minutes or until the pudding thickens.

Garnish with the pistachio nuts and serve hot.

Variation: For a lighter version of this dish, more appropriate for serving at breakfast, heat the milk and stir in the sugar, saffron, crushed green cardamom pods and sultanas, omitting the cream. Do not simmer for 30 minutes. Instead, add the vermicelli immediately, and then continue as for the recipe above.

Baked Saffron Yoghurt Pudding with Tomato Compote

Serves 4

Sweetened yoghurt, in its many guises, is a popular dessert in Bengal, where the sweet shops are full of little terracotta pots brimming with a caramelised yoghurt. This dish was first made at the Spice Kitchen many years ago, and this particular interpretation of a sweetened yoghurt is all mine. The unusual partnership of tomato and yoghurt works really well.

4 ripe tomatoes, chopped

1 teaspoon ginger paste (page 12)

220 g (8 oz/1 cup) sugar

250 g (9 oz/1 cup) plain yoghurt

160 g (5½ oz/½ cup) sweetened condensed milk

60 ml (2 fl oz/¼ cup) thick (double/heavy) cream

1 teaspoon saffron infusion (page 13)

1 egg, lightly beaten

Preheat the oven to 160°C (320°F).

Mix together the tomato, ginger paste and sugar in a medium saucepan over a medium heat and cook for about 8–10 minutes, or until the tomato has softened. Spread out over the base of a 25 x 12 cm (10 x 4¾ in) ovenproof dish.

Mix together the yoghurt, condensed milk, cream, saffron infusion and egg in a medium bowl.

Pour the yoghurt mixture over the tomato mixture and bake in the oven for 20–35 minutes, or until the pudding is just set. When the pudding is cooked, it will look smooth like a panna cotta, but it will still be a little wobbly. It is important not to cook it for any longer once it reaches this stage, because overcooking will make it curdle and the water separate. (The pudding will become firmer and lose its wobbliness when it is chilled in the refrigerator.)

Chill in the refrigerator for 1 hour, then serve in dessert glasses.

Christmas Kulfi

Serves 6

In many parts of India, just as in most parts of Australia, Christmas is often a beautifully sunny and warm day. Kulfi is a traditional Indian ice cream, and this kulfi recipe is just right after a rich meal in any climate. You can serve it flamed with brandy for a special festive touch.

2 tablespoons unsweetened cocoa powder

315 g (11 oz/1 cup) sweetened condensed milk

375 ml (12½ fl oz/1½ cups) evaporated milk

375 ml (12½ fl oz/1½ cups) thick (double/heavy) cream

3 tablespoons ground almonds

125 g (4½ oz/1 cup) dried fruit and nut mix (trail mix) (see Note)

1 teaspoon mixed spice, using equal parts ground cardamom, ground cloves and ground mace

60 ml (2 fl oz/¼ cup) brandy

fresh berries and cherries to serve

Mix together the cocoa and 2 tablespoons of warm water in a large bowl until the cocoa has dissolved. Add the condensed and evaporated milks, cream, ground almonds, dried fruit and nut mix, mixed spice and brandy, and mix together until well combined.

Pour the mixture into a freezer-proof 1.5 litre (51 fl oz/6 cup) mould or terrine or into six 250 ml (8½ fl oz/1 cup) ramekin or dariole moulds. Cover with plastic wrap and freeze for at least 8 hours.

About 5 minutes before serving, transfer the kulfi to the refrigerator. When ready to serve, turn the kulfi out of the large mould or terrine onto a platter and cut into slices, or invert the individual ramekins onto plates. (If you are having difficulty getting the kulfi out, you can roll the individual ramekins between your hands to provide a little warmth and help remove the kulfi from the ramekins. However, do not run hot water over them as this will make the surface of the ice cream melt.)

Scatter the berries and cherries around the kulfi and serve immediately.

Note: You could buy a ready-made dried fruit and nut mix, or you could make your own, choosing your preferred combination from dried figs, cranberries, apricots, currants, sultanas (golden raisins) and raisins, and nuts such as almonds, pistachio nuts, walnuts and hazelnuts.

Coconut Pancakes

Serves 4

Indian sweets are served not only at the end of the meal, they are eaten as a snack at any time of day! A favourite in Bengal, this is a simple recipe of thin, crepe-like pancakes filled with a juicy coconut filling – a lovely summer mouthful. They are really very easy to cook, and you might find that the pancakes disappear as soon as you make them.

Batter

150 g (5½ oz/1 cup) plain (all-purpose) flour

2 eggs

250–300 ml (8½–10 fl oz) milk

1 tablespoon vegetable or canola oil or 15 g (½ oz) ghee (page 13)

Coconut Filling

2 tablespoons full-cream powdered milk

45 g (1½ oz/½ cup) desiccated (grated dried) coconut

2 tablespoons sugar

100 ml (3½ fl oz) pouring (single/light) cream

To make the batter, sift the flour into a large bowl and make a well in the centre. Add the eggs, 200 ml (7 fl oz) of the milk and the oil or ghee and whisk together to make a thin, smooth batter, adding the remaining milk as necessary to form the right consistency. Rest for 20 minutes.

Meanwhile, make the coconut filling. Mix together the powdered milk, coconut, sugar and cream in a small bowl until the powdered milk has dissolved and the filling is thick and chunky. Set aside.

Heat a medium non-stick frying pan over a medium heat. Pour in a ladleful of the pancake batter and swirl it around to coat the base of the pan, forming a thin crepe-like pancake about 10 cm (4 in) in diameter. Cook for 2 minutes. Flip and cook on the other side for 5–10 seconds. Transfer the pancake to a large plate and leave to cool. Repeat to use up the remaining batter.

When cool, lay each pancake out on a work surface. Place a thin cylinder of coconut filling across the pancake, near the edge that is closest to you, then roll up the pancake to enclose the filling.

Cut each pancake into 3–4 pieces and serve cold.

Gulab Jamun

Serves 4

Literally translating as 'rose olives', gulab jamun are beautifully soft, warm dumplings, soaked in rosewater-imbued syrup, that just melt in the mouth. Almost all Indian restaurants include gulab jamun on the menu. Enjoy them at home at any time, not just after a meal. They are definitely a crowd pleaser.

vegetable or canola oil for deep-frying

chopped shelled pistachio nuts to garnish

Rosewater Syrup
250 g (9 oz) sugar

2–3 drops of rosewater

Dough
100 g (3½ oz/1 cup) full-cream powdered milk

75 g (2½ oz/½ cup) self-raising flour

30 g (1 oz/¼ cup) semolina

250–375 ml (8½–12½ fl oz/ 1–1½ cups) thick (double/ heavy) cream

To make the rosewater syrup, put the sugar and about 500 ml (17 fl oz/2 cups) water in a medium saucepan (the water should just cover the sugar) and cook, stirring, over a high heat until the sugar has dissolved and the liquid starts to bubble, for 5 minutes at the most. Reduce the heat to low and continue cooking for about 20 minutes, or until the sugar syrup is glossy but not too thick. Add the rosewater to just flavour the syrup, then remove from the heat, cover with a lid and keep warm.

Meanwhile, to make the dough, put the powdered milk, flour and semolina in a large bowl and mix well. Make a well in the middle and gradually spoon in 200 ml (7 fl oz) of the cream while working the ingredients together, adding the remaining cream as necessary to form a soft dough.

Roll the dough into small balls that are about the size of a walnut and as smooth as possible – no cracks should be visible.

Heat the oil in a wok or deep-fryer to 170°C (340°F) (see page 15). Deep-fry the balls a few at a time for about 8 minutes, or until golden brown.

Pour the rosewater syrup into a large heatproof shallow bowl. Remove the balls with a slotted spoon or frying spoon, transfer to the bowl and soak in the syrup for at least 1 hour. Serve warm, with the pistachio nuts sprinkled on top.

Note: You can make gulab jamun in advance. Put the balls and syrup in the refrigerator and just before serving, reheat the balls and syrup in a saucepan over a medium heat until hot.

Orange Halwa with Sultanas

Serves 4

Halwas have a Turkish and Middle Eastern ancestry, and many different versions can be found throughout India, some of them truly, uniquely Indian. This halwa, a lovely, warm, citrusy pudding made with semolina in just minutes, is the ultimate winter dessert. It is also perfect for afternoon tea.

60 g (2 oz) ghee (page 13)

125 g (4½ oz/1 cup) semolina

110 g (4 oz/½ cup) sugar

2 tablespoons sultanas (golden raisins)

190 ml (6½ fl oz/¾ cup) freshly squeezed orange juice, from 2–3 oranges

1 tablespoon grated orange zest

125 ml (4 fl oz/½ cup) milk

orange segments to garnish

Heat the ghee in a large frying pan over a medium heat. Cook the semolina, stirring continuously, for about 5 minutes, or until it starts to brown.

Add the sugar and sultanas and cook, stirring, for 1 minute. Add the orange juice and zest and mix together thoroughly, then cook for 2 minutes.

Pour in the milk and cook, stirring vigorously, for 8–10 minutes or until the liquid is completely absorbed.

Garnish with the orange segments and serve hot.

Carrot Halwa

Serves 4

Halwas are enjoyed all over India. Beetroot (beets), zucchini (courgettes), pumpkin (winter squash), lentils and eggs can all be used as the main ingredient. They can be found in many forms but are usually cooked to a rough mash. Eaten warm, they are the closest thing to a pudding, Indian-style. This winter warmer is a North Indian favourite, and you could double or even triple the quantities I've given as it will keep for up to two weeks in the refrigerator. Heat it up just before serving.

310 g (11 oz) grated carrot

500 ml (17 fl oz/2 cups) milk

220 g (8 oz/1 cup) sugar

125 g (4½ oz) ghee (page 13) or unsalted butter

4 green cardamom pods, crushed

100 g (3½ oz/½ cup) full-cream powdered milk

shelled pistachio nuts to garnish

Mix together the carrot and milk in a large heavy-based saucepan over a medium heat. Bring almost to a boil, then reduce the heat to low and cook, stirring occasionally, for about 1 hour, or until the carrot has absorbed all the milk.

Stir in the sugar, increase the heat to medium and cook for 10 minutes, or until the mixture is dry. Stir in the ghee or butter, then cook, stirring occasionally, for 7 minutes, or until the halwa takes on a glossy appearance.

Add the cardamom and powdered milk and stir through to combine well.

Garnish with the pistachios and serve warm.

Mango Kulfi

Serves 4

The most popular of all kulfis, especially outside of India, is mango kulfi. The lush decadence of the mango seems to really match with the luxurious creaminess of the kulfi – it really is an unforgettable combination. Fresh mangoes will give you the best mango kulfi, but if you're craving a reminder of long, hot summers in the middle of winter, you could use canned mango pulp.

2 mangoes or 425 g (15 oz) can mango pulp or mango slices in syrup

315 g (11 oz/1 cup) sweetened condensed milk

375 ml (12½ fl oz/1½ cups) evaporated milk

375 ml (12½ fl oz/1½ cups) thick (double/heavy) cream

1 tablespoon ground almonds

If using the fresh mangoes, peel them and, using a sharp knife, remove all the mango flesh from around the stone. Process in a food processor to form a smooth pulp. If using canned mango slices in syrup, drain well, then process the slices in a food processor to form a smooth pulp.

Transfer the mango pulp to a large bowl. Add the condensed and evaporated milks, cream and ground almonds and mix together until well combined.

Pour the mixture into a freezer-proof 1.5 litre (51 fl oz/6 cup) mould or terrine or into six 250 ml (8½ fl oz/1 cup) ramekins or dariole moulds. Cover with plastic wrap and freeze for at least 8 hours.

About 5 minutes before serving, transfer the kulfi to the refrigerator for 5 minutes. When ready to serve, turn the kulfi out of the large mould or terrine onto a platter and cut into slices, or invert the individual ramekins onto plates. (If you are having difficulty getting the kulfi out, you can roll the individual ramekins between your hands to provide a little warmth and help remove the kulfi from the ramekins. However, do not run hot water over them as this will make the surface of the ice cream melt.) Serve immediately.

INDEX

ACKNOWLEDGEMENTS

'Last night I dreamt I went again to.' – Chocolate City –
*My father's wonderful bedtime story fantasy, which awakened
my food curiosity forever.*

To Sujoy, who always enjoys my cooking.

To Pritika and Chiragh – this book is an edible link to your roots.

To Fiona and Paul – thank you for the opportunity to share my food.

*To Lucy, Bronwyn, Jana, Deb and Beccy, who took a raw rice grain
and polished it into something deliciously enticing.*

*But most of all, to all of you who will share these wonderful recipes
that are an integral part of my world: enjoy not only the food but
also the stories behind them.*

First published in 2013

An SBS book

Published in 2013 by Hardie Grant Books

Hardie Grant Books (Australia)
Ground Floor, Building 1
658 Church Street
Richmond, Victoria 3121
www.hardiegrant.com.au

Hardie Grant Books (UK)
Dudley House, North Suite
34–35 Southampton Street
London WC2E 7HF
www.hardiegrant.co.uk

A Cataloguing-in-Publication entry is available from the catalogue of the
National Library of Australia at www.nla.gov.au.

Spice Kitchen

ISBN 978 1 74270 520 0

Publishing Director: Paul McNally
Managing Editor: Lucy Heaver
Editor: Bronwyn Sweeney
Design Manager: Heather Menzies
Designer: Beccy Brown
Photographer: Jana Liebenstein
Stylist: Deb Kaloper
Production Manager: Todd Rechner

Colour reproduction by Splitting Image Colour Studio
Printed and bound in China by 1010 Printing International Limited

Hardie Grant would like to thank Market Imports, Mud Australia
and Made In Japan for the use of props in this book.